Mark H. Walker

PUBLISHED BY
Microsoft Press
A Division of Microsoft Corporation
One Microsoft Way
Redmond, Washington 98052-6399

Library of Congress Cataloging-in-Publication Data
Walker, Mark (Mark H.)
    Microsoft Age of Empires II : The Conquerors Expansion : Inside Moves / Mark H. Walker.
        p. cm.
    Includes index.
    ISBN 0-7356-1177-7
    1. Microsoft Age of Empires. I. Title: Conquerors Expansion. II. Title: Microsoft Age
of Empires 2. III. Title: Microsoft Age of Empires Two. IV. Title.

GV1469.25.M572 W25 2000
793.93'25369--dc21

                                                        00-057855

Printed and bound in the United States of America.

1 2 3 4 5 6 7 8 9   MLML   5 4 3 2 1 0

Distributed in Canada by Penguin Books Canada Limited.

A CIP catalogue record for this book is available from the British Library.

Microsoft Press books are available through booksellers and distributors worldwide. For further information about international editions, contact your local Microsoft Corporation office or contact Microsoft Press International directly at fax (425) 936-7329. Visit our Web site at mspress.microsoft.com. Send comments to mspinput@microsoft.com.

Acquisitions Editor: Casey Doyle
Project Editor: Sandra Haynes
Manuscript Editor: Devon Musgrave
Technical Editor: Jim Fuchs

Dedication

This book is dedicated to white cake with white icing...
you know, the kind they make in a bakery.

Acknowledgments

I'm very proud of this book. The two walkthroughs per mission and the BattleBits are strategy guide firsts (as far as I know). It took, however, a lot of people to put this unique guide together, and I'd like to thank them. Thanks to my wife, Janice, who has probably taken more Age II screen shots than anyone on the planet. Thanks to Casey Doyle for the work and Sandra Haynes for the excellent project management. Thanks to James McDaniel, a program manager on the Age II team, for all his help during an incredibly busy time. Thanks to Michael "Staffa" Christensen, Dennis Stone, and Matthew Scadding, testers on the Age II team, for their input. Thanks to Jim Fuchs for the technical editing, Devon Musgrave for the manuscript editing, Carl Diltz for the layout, Crystal Thomas for the proofreading and copyediting, and Joel Panchot for the artwork. Thanks to Mark "my ROM works fine" Barrett—freelance writer and game designer whose other credits include mission design for *Fighter Squadron: The Screamin' Demons Over Europe* and the story for *Dark Side of the Moon,* Bart "17K a day" Farkas—noted strategy guide writer and author of *Starcraft: The Official Strategy Guide,* and Michael "the grammar dude" Emberson—who designs sentences with a full range of clauses, adverbs, and other multisyllabic offerings.

Contents

AGE
of
EMPIRES II

PART II   THE CONQUERORS: WALKTHROUGHS AND STRATEGIES   53

AGE _of_ EMPIRES II

PART III   INSIDE MOVES:
INFORMATION YOU WON'T FIND ANYWHERE ELSE   239

AGE *of* EMPIRES II

Introduction

It all started with *Microsoft Age of Empires,* a game that let people guide civilizations within a historical context. For the first time, gamers could play as the ancient Egyptians or one of the Greek cultures, complete with their stylish and unique attributes. In fact, droves of fans—over two million of them—basked in the opportunity to make decisions like the great military strategists Alexander, Cyrus, Darius I, and Nebuchadnezzar II. One civilization, however, was missing. The expansion pack *The Rise of Rome* solved that problem, enabling real-time scenario (RTS) grognards to finally put on their togas and become the Caesar of *Age of Empires.*

People could not get enough of conquering their friends. Ensemble Studios and Microsoft teamed up again in 1999 to produce the blockbuster smash *Microsoft Age of Empires II: The Age of Kings.* This time *Empires* had gone Medieval. Rome is in shambles, giving way to warring factions and splintered kingdoms; stone castles replace marble colonnades; and Christianity and Islam are sweeping the Occident, culminating in the Crusades. Gamers were enthralled by this new age of epic combat. In re-creating history, Ensemble and Microsoft made history themselves, giving birth to a RTS empire of their own. The latest installment in their franchise, the expansion pack *Microsoft Age of Empires II: The Conquerors,* adds to this legacy with new civilizations and features.

Setting the Stage: The Premise of *The Conquerors*

The Age of Kings begins with the dissolution of Rome and proceeds to the European Renaissance, focusing on the Middle Ages (500–1500 CE). *The Conquerors* features some of the major civilizations not included in the *Empires* sequel. For example, the powerful and devastating Huns now get their chance to wreak havoc on Europe—just as they did 1500 years ago. One of the campaigns even gives ruthless conquerors the chance to walk in mighty Attila's footsteps. The early Renaissance is also well represented in the expansion pack. During the early sixteenth century, New World exploration quickly developed into new conquests. Along with the Spanish (as shown in Figure I-1), two Mesoamerican civilizations—the Aztecs and the Mayans—appear in the expansion pack. The Koreans, the fifth new civilization, join the rank of Far Eastern kingdoms. As *The Rise of Rome* completed the first *Age of Empires*, *The Conquerors* gives more breadth to *The Age of Kings*.

Figure I-1   *Spanish Conquistadors and Missionaries (Monks on horseback) are among some of the new units in the expansion pack.*

What's New in the Expansion Pack

The Conquerors no doubt completes the sequel, but it's about far more than just new civilizations. Microsoft and Ensemble provide four new campaigns (including Attila, Montezuma, and El Cid), 11 new units, 26 new technologies, 10 real-world maps (such as Britain, Central America, Italy, and Texas), and three new game types (King of the Hill, Wonder Race, and Defend the Wonder). Tropical and winter terrain is available, the former including man-hungry Jaguars, the latter's snow letting you hunt down enemies by following their tracks. Ensemble Studios has also made enhancements to the game engine, creating smarter Villagers (as shown in Figure I-2), improving trading and tributes, allowing ships to be placed in formations, and giving gamers the ability to garrison infantry and foot Archers to Rams. But this is just the tip of the iceberg.

Overall, the expansion packs offers a plethora of new features. Ensemble Studios has made a number of key changes to the original *Age of Kings* civilizations. Many of the game's original units have also seen changes. Modifications include Hand Cannoneers with an increased attack vs. infantry, Samurai and Woad Raiders with armor piercing ability, Relics that generate more Gold, Outposts with increased line of sight, and Town Centers that cost 275 Wood and 100 Stone (instead of just 275 Wood). Check out the package material for *The Conquerors* for more details on the game's changes.

Figure I-2   *Smarter Villagers require less micromanaging, letting you take care of more important strategies.*

Note: *Villagers are now less prone to slack off on the job. For example, after constructing a Lumber Camp, a Villager automatically chops Wood. When finished erecting a structure, a Villager assists his neighbors on their construction project—without your intervention.*

This Book's Audience

This strategy guide is designed for all levels of *Age of Empires II* players, including veterans, novices, and those in between. Special emphasis, however, is placed on gamers who have some real-time strategy game experience but do not consider themselves experts. If you're having problems beating the computer when playing at high difficulty levels or you're being schooled on the Zone, this book can improve your game in leaps and bounds. More experienced players will get their money's worth from the advanced economic and military strategies, many of which will be shown in the BattleBits section. Besides tactics for the new civilizations and new game types, you'll find plenty of notes and tips along with not one but two walkthroughs for every campaign mission.

Note: *Seven of the original Age of Kings civilizations have attribute changes. The Britons' Town Centers cost 50 percent less Wood only during the Castle Age. The Byzantines' Team Bonus consists of Monks healing 50 percent faster instead of three times normal speed. The Chinese now start with –50 Wood along with the original –150 Food. Goth Hunters carry +15 meat. Teutonic Town Centers have +5 line of sight instead of +5 range. The Turks' Hussar upgrade is free and gunpowder units have +25 Hit Points instead of +50 percent. Finally, Viking Docks cost –25 percent instead of –33 percent.*

How the Book Is Organized

This book is laid out in a simple and easy-to-use manner. Part I, "Civilization-Specific Strategies For *Age of Empires* II: The Conquerors Expansion," contains five chapters with information about the five new cultures: the Aztecs, Huns, Koreans, Mayans, and Spanish. Each chapter is devoted to a particular civilization, featuring a short history along with in-depth commentaries, tips, and tactics based on each culture's special attributes, units, and technologies.

Part II, "The Conquerors: Walkthroughs and Strategies," supplies more meat for Empire-builders to feast upon. Chapters 6 through 9 contain campaign walkthroughs, including those for the stand-alone scenarios. (See Figure I-3.) Chapter 10 provides basic strategies for winning the three new game types in *The Conquerors*. Multiplayer fans will find what they need in Chapter 11, from tips on the game's new maps to how to use the latest features in all 18 of the civilizations to your advantage.

Part III, "Inside Moves: Information You Won't Find Anywhere Else," contains information that you won't find anywhere else, including BattleBits, strategies from some of the game's testers, and a list of notable *Age of Empires II* Web sites. If you're searching for in-depth advice and tactics, look no more. Just read on.

Figure I-3 *William the Conqueror leads the Normans in the battle of Hastings, one of the game's campaign stand-alone missions.*

PART I

Civilization-Specific Strategies for *Age of Empires II: The Conquerors Expansion*

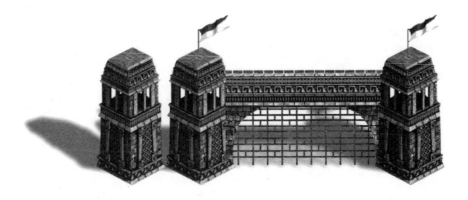

Chapter One

The Aztecs: Background, Strategy, and Tactics

The Aztecs of North America flourished between the fourteenth and sixteenth centuries in what is now central Mexico. Founding the city of Tenochtitlan around 1325 on the current site of Mexico City, the Aztecs extended their influence to neighboring villages and tribes. A dominant empire during that time, the Aztec civilization was sustained by conquest, tribute, and religious sacrifice. The Aztecs believed a number of gods dictated the events of the day and that they needed to honor and appease those gods regularly. To do so, Aztec priests sacrificed members of the society in the belief that cutting the beating hearts from their victims' chests would secure their empire. (Not to dwell on this subject, but if you're interested in the Aztec methods for this sacrifice—which varied with culture, context, and victim—look up midaxial thoracotomy, transversal thoracotomy, and what's called the intercostal approach.)

The most familiar Aztec leader is Montezuma II (1480–1520), who ruled beginning in 1502 through a series of disasters and bad omens—including heavy rains, a comet, three earthquakes, and cold weather (and its resultant crop failures and famine)—and during 1519 when the Spanish arrived. Believing the Spanish leader, Hernando Cortez, to be an incarnation of the god Quetzalcoatl returning as told in legend to retake his lands, Montezuma II presented Cortez with ornate gold and silver gifts, which only fueled Cortez's desire to conquer and plunder the Aztec civilization. Cortez eventually took Montezuma hostage in 1520, but the Aztecs revolted at this attempt to control them and killed Montezuma when he tried to address them at the request of the Spaniards. (By the way, there are variants to the story of Montezuma's

death. It's also thought that the Spanish slit Montezuma's throat when retreating from the Aztec capital.) The Aztecs waged a bitter war against Spanish rule for a few more years until their civilization's collapse.

Aztec Attributes

Although relatively primitive, the might at Montezuma's command was considerable and well adapted to the ways of the jungle. By learning these attributes well and taking advantage of them in the field, you'll make it difficult for even the most technologically advanced army to defeat you.

Unique Unit: Jaguar Warrior

The Jaguar Warrior—upgradeable to the Elite Jaguar Warrior—is a powerful infantry unit with an attack bonus against enemy infantry. Heavily armored, the Jaguar Warriors are a disruptive force against even the most dedicated defensive lines and are particularly potent when you transport them in Rams.

Unique Technology: Garland Wars
(+4 Infantry Attack, +6 Attack vs. Cavalry)

Befitting a civilization without horses, Garland Wars expresses the Aztec civilization's expertise at infantry combat and the toll the dense jungle took on its enemies. A considerable bonus for the already deadly Jaguar Warrior, Garland Wars even turns a Spearman (and its upgrades) into a terror. Garland Wars should be one of the main objectives of any Aztec leader.

Team Bonus: Relics +33 Percent Gold

Well known for its abundant supply of Gold, the Aztec civilization produces an additional amount when a Relic is installed in a Shrine (Monastery). Although not applicable to all situations, a Shrine with even one Relic can keep the Aztecs alive while enemies run short of funds. (See Figure 1-1.)

No Cavalry— Eagle Scouts Instead

In keeping with the absence of cavalry of any kind in the Aztec civilization, the Eagle Warrior unit (upgradeable at the Barracks to Elite Eagle Warrior) replaces the Scout Cavalry unit. With a long line of sight and considerable speed, the Eagle Warrior is more than a replacement; it is an advantageous unit to command.

Figure 1-1   *Seizing two Relics and shipping them home will pay big dividends before the battle is over.*

Villagers Carry +5 More

Another acknowledgment of the Aztec ability to derive needed resources from the rich jungle surroundings, this Villager bonus adds up very quickly, particularly when you deploy a large number of Villagers early. In addition, this bonus allows you to postpone normal Villager upgrades and put military preparations on the front burner from the beginning.

All Military Units Created 15 Percent Faster

Also a considerable bonus when used with greater frequency, this attribute allows you to counter the greater individual strength of enemy units with a more resilient force. In a battle of attrition, this restorative bonus could make the difference between victory and defeat.

Monks +5 Hit Points for Each Monastery Technology

A nod to the spiritual center that was the Aztec empire, this advantage can either obviate the need for researching Sanctity or make it that much more powerful. Although a possible inducement to improve the power of Priests (Monks), this bonus will most naturally occur as a matter of course and still deliver considerable benefits.

Aztec Strategies

As an Aztec leader, you must fully appreciate what infantry can and cannot do. Because the infantry lacks the speed advantage of mounted units and their heavy armor, to command the infantry wisely, you must pay particularly close attention to where and when you fight a battle. With deliberate and careful planning and the application of *all* the forces at your disposal, you'll reap a bloody harvest from what you sow.

Although the Aztec infantry is powerful and can be made even stronger, you must not overlook some limitations. Against some siege weapons, all infantry are vulnerable, and groups of infantry more so (although using the Staggered formation mitigates this vulnerability). Also, the strength of an infantry unit decreases rapidly when isolated. This duality makes it difficult to know when to lead large groups of infantry on the attack.

The solution is to learn which units your enemy is fielding by engaging in reconnaissance before you join a battle. For this and other purposes, the Eagle Warrior is an ideal choice and can cover a good deal of territory in a short amount of time. Although not the strongest offensive unit, the Eagle Warrior adeptly takes on Archers and other noninfantry ground units, which also makes it a good complement to the Jaguar Warrior.

In the end, however, it's likely that thoroughly upgraded infantry will carry the day, and although Garland Wars is the centerpiece of the strengthening process, take care not to overlook the mundane advances available at the Blacksmith. Finally, your Jaguar and Eagle Warriors are special, but don't forget

your regular infantry, which can achieve feats in battle equal to those of your unique Aztec units.

Aztec Tactics

Because of the limitations of your forces, you must proceed with care. Maneuvering is not one of the foot soldiers' strengths, so you need to win battles in the planning stages. Though lacking the fireworks of an all-out assault, a vision executed with the following techniques yields more than compensatory rewards.

Patience

Although aggression is important on the battlefield, exercising tactical patience wins at least as many victories. With an infantry-heavy force ill suited to disengaging in the middle of battle, seize the *best* opportunity to attack rather than the *first*.

Resource Management

The tactical ability of any army depends on the ready availability of necessary resources. It stands to reason, then, that making sure your Aztec units are well supported and anticipating changes in available resources are important parts of readiness. To wisely choose *when* to fight, you must first know you will be *able* to fight.

City Management

Treating each build-up as a process unique to every new conflict is as important as making an assessment about the lay of the land you'll be transiting. No expense or decision is too trivial to consider against the cost of readiness. You must constantly reevaluate the importance of upgrades, areas of research, and buildings.

Unit Management

Because you have less armor, speed, and firepower than other civilizations, you must carefully construct the Aztec infantry in regards to number and type. An unfavorable application of force against an enemy can be a disaster from which there is no reprieve. Also, consider ramping up production so that sheer numbers substitute for quality. There are few substitutions for numbers, especially in the early game. Remember: sophisticated warriors under research cannot defend nor attack. You must put troops on the battlefield. Sometime this means hordes of "low-tech" units.

Defense

It is an established truth that it takes three attackers to route one defender. For the leader with limited firepower and limited mobility, this adage gives a clear

signal about how to respond to a threat. Far from being a timid act, mounting a good defense can erode an attacking army more quickly than a counterattack can and helps to leave defensive forces in condition for an assault in the aftermath. (See Figure 1-2.)

Figure 1-2   *Against a primitive enemy, one Onager and a Stone Wall may be all you need for defense.*

Reconnaissance

As the Aztec leader, you need to gain knowledge to use to your advantage. To choose your own battleground, you must know where the enemy is and the terrain features in the area. (See Figure 1-3.) Without excellent and updated reconnaissance, you should remain on the defensive and avoid the temptation to guess.

Containment

Because the Aztec force's maneuverability is limited, seek to inhibit the enemy's mobility as well. Whether by engaging in street fighting or by restricting the enemy to a single avenue of access, try to limit your opponents' advantages by constricting the battlefield around them.

Figure 1-3   *Eagle Warriors make excellent scouts.*

The Decoy

Fast and resilient against Archers, the Eagle Warrior is almost a perfect scout. When sped among defensive units, a lone Eagle Warrior can cross an enemy compound almost unharmed and in so doing draw numerous defenders and sentries away from their posts. (See Figure 1-4.)

Figure 1-4   *Although being damaged, the Eagle Warrior is drawing away numerous enemy defenders.*

Figure 1-5   *The Mayan Archers will have almost no effect on the Rams as they level the Mayan city.*

The Lure

Always attempt to lure the enemy to the most advantageous battleground rather than take on the enemy where they stand. By luring an opponent into a conflict, particularly if it appears imminent in any case, you can seize the initiative in a passive, or even defensive, manner.

Rams

When loaded with infantry, Rams gain considerable speed, which makes them good conveyances for long distances. Also, because Rams have superior resistance to Archers, you can use them to ferry more susceptible units to point-blank range or through contested territory. (See Figure 1-5.)

Ships

Like Rams, transports help make up for the limited mobility of

infantry and siege weapons. In addition, Fire Ships and War Galleys not only can support loaded transports to their destinations but in and of themselves can contest shorelines against small enemy bands or single units. (See Figure 1-6.)

Combined Arms

A good mix of units is particularly important in an infantry formation. Whereas other forces might choose to fight or flee, the infantry must accept the battle they join. Whether by adding an Eagle Warrior to a formation to increase its line of sight or by adding Priests to aid survivability, you should always mix units to the greatest advantage and to present the smallest risk.

Figure 1-6 *Simply by their presence, these ships control the river and pose a threat.*

Combined Attacks

Because it's not always possible to remain on the defensive or to choose the field of battle, be prepared to mount an offensive with combined attacks. Try placing siege weapons or Archers on the flanks to hem in the enemy while sending Priests to steal into the enemy's rear areas to convert key buildings. By combining attack tactics, you can accomplish feats that you could not achieve with only one tactic.

Despite having limited available forces, you should not assume as the Aztec leader that you have limited tactical choices. The choices are simply different, and accepting the differences, rather than fighting them, is the key to victory.

Chapter Two

The Huns: Background, Strategy, and Tactics

Writing late in the fourth century A.D., Roman historian Ammianus Marcellinus described the diet of the Huns as "roots that they find in the fields and the half-raw flesh of any animal." He went on to say, "I say 'half-raw' because they give it a kind of cooking by placing it between their own thighs and the backs of their horses." Long before Attila rose to power as the Huns' king in 433 or 434 A.D., the Huns were a powerful and dangerous nomadic people who had already beaten the Ostrogoths and Visigoths and who had tested the strength of the Roman Empire's northeastern borders. By the 420s, the empire's Eastern Emperor was paying the Huns an annual subsidy to maintain an uneasy alliance. But even doubling that subsidy would not satisfy Attila, who soon eyed, attacked, and conquered much of the Western Roman Empire. Attila's strength grew to rival, and ultimately to cast a shadow over, that of the Roman Empire itself.

Attila was ruthless, cruel, and chillingly effective. (Research his defeat of the city of Naissus in 441 for a particularly bloody example.) Yet, although famous in his own time and ours for his armies' pillaging and plunder, Attila was also a resourceful tactician and strategist. He battled the mighty Roman war machine more than once, under varying circumstances, and always gave as good as he got. In the Attila the Hun campaign, your task is to breathe even more life into the Hunnic forces, using them to the best advantage against forces more powerful and heavily armed than your own. (Note that this was not always the case in Attila's actual campaigns. Sometimes his forces easily outnumbered those of his foes. Estimates of his army's size when invading Gaul range between 300,000 and 700,000 soldiers.) If you can use your strengths wisely and minimize the effects of your weaknesses, you will walk in the footsteps of Attila himself and bring the Roman Empire to its knees.

Hun Attributes

The Huns have a number of special attributes derived from the skills of the forces that plundered central Europe under Attila's command. Understanding and using their special attributes and units to best advantage is the key to Hunnic victory.

Unique Unit: Tarkan

The Tarkan—upgradeable to the Elite Tarkan—is more than just another Cavalry unit. (See Figure 2-1.) With an attack bonus against buildings, a column of Tarkans is a wrecking machine equal in might to the most formidable siege engines but with the added advantage of speed. Able to charge in and destroy a tower or building and then turn and retreat in an instant, a Tarkan column is like no other force in the game.

Figure 2-1   *Think of the Tarkans as human siege weapons. Their quickness makes them one of the most dangerous units in the game.*

Unique Technology: Atheism

Atheism doubles the amount of time necessary for enemies to achieve a Wonder or Relic victory, and it halves the cost of Spies or Treason. A reflection of the terror the Huns made their foes feel, this technology can change the course of a battle in a single stroke. Combined with the attacking power of the Tarkans, Atheism greatly decreases the likelihood that an enemy will achieve victory without first shedding considerable blood.

Team Bonus: Stables 20 Percent Faster

The Hun team bonus reflects the Hunnic mastery of the horse. Producing units 20 percent faster, the Stable brings Cavalry, Knights, and their upgrades into play at a breakneck pace. Welcome complements to the Tarkans, these mounted units can easily keep up with the Huns' unique unit, taking on other enemy forces while the Tarkans raze enemy structures.

No Houses Required

As a result of their no-madic lifestyle, the Huns do not have to build houses to support more units. (See Figure 2-2.) Combined with the improved Stable production and Conscription (available at the Castle), this special attribute allows a mounted army to be generated in short order.

Figure 2-2   *Huns are nomadic conquerors and have little use for Houses. Wherever the Huns roam is home.*

AGE *of* EMPIRES II

Cavalry Archer Cost Reduced

In keeping with the preference for mounted units, the Huns also get an edge with the Cavalry Archer, which costs −25 percent during the Castle Age and −30 percent during the Imperial Age. Another fast mounted unit, the Cavalry Archer provides ranged backup to the more powerful Knights and Tarkans.

Trebuchets +30 Percent Accuracy

Reflecting the Hunnic expertise at plundering objectives, Hun Trebuchets are +30 percent in accuracy with every shot. Damage is inflicted not only more consistently but also more quickly, allowing Hun Trebuchets to be deployed, fired, and recovered before enemy foot soldiers can arrive on the scene (See Figure 2-3.)

Figure 2-3   *Trebuchets, because of their accuracy and speed, tend to last longer in battle.*

Hun Strategies

One thing defines the Hun forces: mobility. The speed with which the Huns can attack, recover, defend, and maneuver is unparalleled, and they can easily wreak havoc on stronger but slower units and forces. By attacking in withering, lightning-quick advances and then withdrawing with equal speed, the Huns inflict grievous wounds and confusion, while at the same time limiting the damage to themselves. Also adept at luring

unsuspecting forces afield from behind battlements and from within city walls, the Huns are capable of an array of feints and diversions aimed at confusing enemy defenses.

Quick sack-and-burn raids are what the Huns do best. (See Figure 2-4.) Pulling your forces out as enemy forces begin gathering in numbers is the se-

cret to commanding the Hunnic army. Regardless of the nature of the battle, the Hun leader should always try to preserve his force's mobility. Entrenched fronts and long drawn out battles serve the enemy and should be avoided at all cost.

On the defensive, the Huns must not become passive or superior enemy strength will carry the day. To be effective, even on the defensive, mounted units should remain mobile and aggressive, seek-

Figure 2-4   *The Huns's agility makes them ideal for hit-and-run ambushes on enemy structures.*

ing to engage those parts of the attacking enemy force over which they have an advantage. By selectively engaging the enemy's forces and using speed to reach rear units, the Hunnic horde can disrupt even the most disciplined attack.

Hun Tactics

Springing from the mobility of the Hun army and grounded in the strategy of selective engagement, the following tactics are certain to vex your enemies.

Evasion

The simple fact that a unit is moving significantly reduces its risk when under fire. Note the Cavalry running from the Archers in Figure 2-5. For units moving as fast as a mount, the risk becomes almost negligible, even in the midst of enemy forces. For these reasons, Hunnic forces should always be on the move, evading both enemy units and enemy fire. Civilizations that cannot research Thumb Ring have a particularly difficult time bringing down fast mounted forces. These include, among others, the Britons, Franks, Goths, and Teutons, as shown in Figure 2-5.

Figure 2-5   *Gothic Archers, a common historical foe of the Huns, will have a tougher time reaching your cavalry units than those that have Thumb Ring technology.*

Hit-and-Run

The ultimate Hun tactic, the Hit-and-Run approach to warfare frustrated opponents by eliminating a clear front upon which grand designs could be made. Without established territory to protect, and without fixed or ponderous defenses, the Huns were free to attack where they wanted when they so chose. Consider both sequential Hit-and-Run attacks on multiple targets or repeated attacks on the same target over time.

Disengagement

Akin to Hit-and-Run, the ability to disengage from battle at a pivotal moment is
not an option for many forces. For the Huns, however, it is a potent ploy. Not
only can disengagement frustrate your opponent and give you time to regroup,
but it can lead to opportunistic Hit-and-Run attacks if the enemy has weakened
its defenses to meet the current threat.

Retreat

The mounted Huns always have the option of retreat—an orderly response to
an overwhelming force—as a tactical response. Far from an admission of defeat, a Hunnic retreat should instead be an attempt to change the location of a
battle for advantage—victory being the goal. Mobility is again key, allowing the
Huns to reverse their steps before the enemy can cut them off, as shown in
Figure 2-6. Some retreats have deliberate aims, such as the Retreat to Arms, Retreat to Safety, and Retreat to Heal, all mentioned below.

Retreat to Arms

An intentional attempt
to bring slower mov-
ing or fixed Hun units
into the fray, a Retreat
to Arms involves dis-
engaging from a battle
and regrouping on
ground occupied by,
or soon to be taken
by, slower Hun forces.
This retreat has the
advantage of depriv-
ing the enemy of the
same opportunity,
should the tide turn
against that enemy,
because no other
army in the world can
outrun the Huns in
retreat.

Figure 2-6 *Huns on the run. When all else fails, retreat from the enemy. With your speed, they won't be able to catch you.*

Retreat to Safety

An attempt to shelter a formation against overwhelming odds, the Retreat to Safety seeks to make use of fixed defenses for support. Because Hun mounts can usually outdistance their foes, an orderly retreat of this kind buys time, which in turn aids in the creation or redeployment of defensive units and structures as well as in the strengthening of the retreating formation.

Retreat to Heal

An admission of temporary defeat, the Retreat to Heal seeks to return wounded units and forces to locations where they can recover. (See Figure 2-7.) Although a Monk or Castle is little help to a mounted force on the attack, they are a great help when stationed in "regrouping points" behind defensive battles. By retreating at opportune times and healing, the Huns gain the advantage of superior health and save the time and resources needed to build replacements.

Figure 2-7   *Use your Monks to heal wounded units.*

The Feint

Running a band of Archers at a city gate is an invitation to disaster and a feint without substance because the Archers can do no damage. With the Tarkans, however, the Hun leader has the ability to make a determined and concerted feint in force, a feint that few enemies can afford to ignore. Whether used to buy time or to distract the enemy and pull his forces out of position, a Tarkan feint normally incurs few losses.

The Decoy

Hun mounted units' speed and power make them excellent decoys, as shown in Figure 2-8. It's hard for opposing forces to ambush or trap such an elusive force, and enemy forces that do pursue often end up strung out, negating their combined arms advantages. Once disrupted, these forces are at considerable disadvantage, and any that remain a threat can simply be avoided while attention is turned to those that are now vulnerable.

Figure 2-8 *Use decoys for defensive purposes, too. For example, station a few cavalry units near your Lumber Camps. These will distract roaming invaders from instantly attacking your lumberjacks.*

The Rush

Once a gate or wall has been breached, the ability to quickly pour troops inside can shatter otherwise sound defenses. Once inside the perimeter, slow-moving units will struggle to run down and engage the Huns, even with ranged weapons, and might find themselves being led in circles. Equally useful on the field of battle, a good Rush against Siege Engines or Monks can turn an offensive force into one fighting for its life.

Demolition

Tarkans are not unlike Petards in their destructive capability. Unlike Petards, however, the Tarkans' mobility means that even a Siege Onager is useless against them if they are bent on reaching a guarded target. Even Guard Towers, although potent, can also usually be destroyed in a matter of moments without losing a single Tarkan—particularly if damaged units are withdrawn to a safe distance while the others fight on.

Combined Arms

While still maintaining speed and mobility, Hun units can be combined into devastating formations. (See Figure 2-9.) Tarkans paired with Knights, Hussars, or other cavalry are potent, but the teaming of cavalry and Cavalry Archers is almost unstoppable. With a front rank of cavalry and two rear ranks of Cavalry Archers, the formation acts like a fast-moving wall upon which enemy units crash as a hail of arrows brings them down.

Figure 2-9   *This is an ideal Hun formation for attacking enemy troops.*

Timed Attacks

Given all of the above, it stands to reason that if any one Hun formation can pose a threat, multiple formations or armies using combined arms would be horrific to encounter. By throwing Hussars and Cavalry Archers at an enemy and then charging them from another direction with Tarkans, enemy forces and positions can be crushed with frightening speed. Timed attacks also mean that the enemy will always be engaging healthy troops, while your damaged forces are withdrawn to heal.

Many of these tactics are not unique to the Huns. What is unique is the Huns' ability to perform all of these maneuvers at speed, often over distances that preclude immediate counterattack. This mobility is the cornerstone of the Hunnic threat. Use it to your advantage, and make ol' Attila proud. (See Figure 2-10.)

Figure 2-10   *The legendary Attila appears in a campaign.*

Chapter Three

The Koreans: Background, Strategy, and Tactics

Korea's location plays a large role in its rich history. Situated on a large Asian peninsula between the Yellow Sea (off the coast of China) and the Sea of Japan, the country quickly became one of the area's booming trade centers. This wealth and activity had a price, though: the country found itself frequently attacked by its imperialistic neighbors, including the Jurchen of Manchuria, the Jin and Song Chinese, and the Mongols. Korea, however, managed to maintain its independence throughout much of the medieval period, due primarily to a strong navy and its political savvy.

The Koreans originated as a group of splintered and warring tribes. However, by the latter half of the seventh century, these tribes began to unite, finding strength in numbers against Chinese forces. By 918, the entire peninsula was consolidated into three kingdoms (known as the Later Three Kingdoms): Silla, Later Paekche, and Koryo (from which the name "Korea" came). Wang Kon, leader of the Koryo dynasty, united these kingdoms in 936, and the dynasty ruled to 1388, fending off attacks from Mongolia, China, Japan, and Manchuria. The Choson (Yi) dynasty that replaced the Koryo thwarted Japanese invaders in the Imjin Wars with the innovative Korean Turtle Ship (Kobukson), the first ironclad vessel in history. The Choson kingdom's rule, like that of the Turkish Ottoman Empire, extended far beyond the times of *Age of Empires II* into the early twentieth century.

Korean Attributes

As a result of their history, the Koreans have many units and features geared toward defensive strategies. In particular, special tower attributes and heavily armored Turtle Ships are excellent for fending off opponents on both land and sea. However, the Koreans are not shabby either when putting together offensive fronts. A second unique unit, the War Wagon, along with special siege attributes enable this civilization to mount some devastating attacks.

Unique Unit #1: Turtle Ship

This ironclad vessel—famous for helping the Koreans, led by Admiral Yi Sunsin, beat back a Japanese onslaught—is available at Docks after you erect a Castle. Although slow, the Turtle Ship's fair range and armor give opponents headaches. The Korean vessel, shown in Figure 3-1, has a distinct advantage at sea, offering more Hit Points than any other ship in the game, including the Galleon and the Vikings' Elite Longboat. In fact, of all mobile units, only the Persian War Elephants have more Hit Points than the Turtle Ship. With the *Conquerors Expansion* ship formation capabilities, this boat's size and durability make it an excellent front-line vessel in defensive and—remember—offensive situations. The Elite Turtle Ship upgrade is available in the Imperial Age.

Figure 3-1 *Turtle Ships are excellent for defending Docks from enemy assaults.*

Unique Unit #2: War Wagon

The Koreans are one of only three civilizations with two unique units. (The others are the Spanish and the Vikings.) The War Wagon, created at the Castle, is the Koreans' other unit, the most powerful Cavalry Archer in the game. Its Hit Points are comparable to those of the Paladin and the Huns' Tarkans. The

Elite War Wagon, an upgrade offered in the Castle Age, has a longer range than the War Wagon. The deadly combination of greater Hit Points and increased firing range gives the Koreans an advantage against new units such as the Hussar, the Eagle Warrior, and the Huns' Tarkan. The Byzantine Cataphracts, Saracen Mamelukes, and French Throwing Axemen also have a difficult time dealing with the War Wagon rampage.

> **Note:** *The Koreans have perhaps the most capable archers in* Age of Empires II. *Along with the powerful War Wagon and access to all basic Archery Range units and technologies (except Parthian Tactics), only the Mongols, Mayans, and Britons rival them in archery strength.*

Unique Technology: Shinkichon

Shinkichon is a ballistic siege technology unique to the Korean civilization. The feature, when researched at the Castle, increases Mangonel range +2. Once implemented, the Bombard Cannon is the only weapon the Korean Siege Workshop produces with a longer firing distance. Be sure to use this advantage in several Castle Age attacks. Mangonel range is further improved in team play.

Team Bonus: Mangonels & Onagers +1 Range

The Koreans' Team Bonus is a perfect complement to the civilization's unique technology. Mangonels, in conjunction with Shinkichon, have an increased total range of +3. However, Onagers only have a +1 total increase. Thus, in these cases, Mangonel range exceeds that of the Imperial Age Onagers. Upgrading to the Onager is still usually a good idea because of its increase in Hit Points and Attack Strength.

Villagers +2 Line of Sight

All Korean Villagers have better eyesight than their counterparts, an advantage for gathering resources and fleeing from intruders. Villagers, for instance, can spot Sheep, Deer, and Forage Berries more quickly than Villagers from other civilizations can. This makes it easier in the opening stages of a game to find nearby resources with your Villagers, which frees your Scout Cavalry to concentrate on monitoring the enemy. In particular, the extra line of sight (LOS) is invaluable for controlling unclaimed sheep, an aspect of the game dependent upon a Shepherd's LOS. (See Figure 3-2.) Furthermore, the increased LOS enables Villagers to spot enemies more quickly, allowing them to escape from the enemy to safety.

Figure 3-2 *Korean Villagers can grab Sheep more quickly because of their increased LOS.*

Stone Miners Work 20 Percent Faster

Although not a requirement for Age advancement, Stone is a critical resource for building several structures, such as walls, towers, Castles, and Wonders. Its importance, in light of the Koreans' attributes, is obvious. Without Stone, taking advantage of the country's unique units (only possible after erecting a Castle) and special tower features is impossible. Although Miners from most

civilizations need to gather Stone as soon as they hit the Feudal Age, Korean Stone Miners can hold out just a bit longer and be okay. Used in conjunction with other economic technologies, such as Wheel-barrow, Hand Cart, and Stone Shaft Mining, the Miners give you the best rock quarry in the game.

> **Note:** *Korean Stone Miners automatically work much faster than those from other countries do. In fact, they are 5 percent quicker than other kingdoms' Miners after those civilizations have researched Stone Mining!*

Tower Upgrades Free

Koreans do not need research to upgrade their towers. When you advance to the next Age, you automatically have access to the latest Tower structure. (See Figure 3-3.) For example, after advancing to the Imperial Age, a Villager can build Keeps instead of Guard Towers without research at a University. Bombard Towers require Chemistry research but, of course, no Bombard Tower research. The free up-grades are a boon in two ways. First, you save on resources that your opponents must spend to make these upgrades—a total of 1400 Food and 1000 Stone from Dark Age to Imperial Age. Second, your opponents must waste time

Figure 3-3   *No research times mean quicker posts at important sites such as Gold Mines.*

collecting these resources and then later researching the Towers. Meanwhile, you can use the extra time and food to strengthen defenses and create more troops.

Increased Tower Range in Castle and Imperial Ages

More Tower Power! The Koreans have +1 tower range in the Castle Age and a total of +2 range in the Imperial Age. The increased distance is an advantage against numerous units, giving the towers more opportunities to shoot at approaching enemies.

Tip: *Early in the game, place towers near occupied and unoccupied Gold and Stone Mines. This thwarts opponents attempts to sift through resources. Furthermore, with the increased range, your towers have the advantage against all other enemy structures. For example, if erected at the right distance, your towers can get free shots at enemy Castles and towers, structures whose limited range prevents them from retaliating.*

Korean Strategies

Playing as the Koreans is not as difficult as with other civilizations. Overall, the kingdom has more strengths than weaknesses. Specifically, a lot of technologies and units are at its disposal—you're not fighting, so to speak, with one arm tied against your back. In particular, good defenses free up novices, which gives them time to gather resources and create a strong offensive threat. More experienced Empire builders should dominate the game from the get-go because of the early opportunities the Koreans afford them.

The Koreans have four military strengths, features that you must use to compensate for two weaknesses (that is, deficient Monk powers and a less-than-stellar cast of Stable and Barracks units). Their strengths are as follows:

- Turtle Boats, with their Hit Points and decent range, make defending your coastline on water maps easy. They're also great for escorting Fishing Ships, Transport Ships, and Trade Cogs.
- Towers enable you to protect your village, scattered resources, and un-claimed Relics from opponents. Use them for offensive attacks, too.

- Archers, especially the War Wagons and Elite War Wagons, are an excellent complement for your melee cavalry forces, which unfortunately lack Bloodlines technology as well as Camel and Paladin units.
- Attributes that increase Mangonel/Onager range give you an important advantage in Castle and Imperial Age offensive strategies.

Keep these features in mind when playing as the Koreans. They are the keys to your success.

Managing resources is not difficult with the Koreans' strong defenses. Their towers are what the doctor ordered to thwart the Huns' aggressive hit-and-run assaults. After you get a handle on your resources and put down several attacks, advancement through the Ages is a cinch. If you're playing a Standard contest, you want to knock out your opponent in the Castle Age, the period in which the Koreans really shine. (Turtle Ships, War Wagons, and Mangonels become available at this time.) The Imperial Age is a bit of a let-down because the Koreans lack powerful units, such as the Paladins and Elite Cannon Galleons. Their defenses, though, make building and defending a Wonder a viable option. (See Figure 3-4.) The Monks' Fervor is also good for gathering Relics. Moreover, Wonder Race and Defend the Wonder are also excellent game types for the Koreans because of the civilization's tower strengths and stone-collecting abilities.

Figure 3-4   *The Koreans build and defend Wonders efficiently.*

Korean Tactics

Concentrating on the four military strengths mentioned previously, use the following tactics to get the most out of the expansion pack's sole addition to the Far Eastern civilizations in *Age of Empires II*.

The Terrible Twin Towers

No game you play as the Koreans is complete without erecting plenty of towers. Free upgrades and increased ranges in the last two Ages make this a must. Always try to erect a pair of towers to complement one another (as shown in Figure 3-5) so that when an enemy horde attacks one tower, the other freely flails spears down upon the assailants. This prevents you from dispatching mobile units to clean things up. Place towers near resources and walls but also stick them at opponents' gates to wound enemy Villagers and military units as they enter and exit their compound.

Figure 3-5   *Plant two towers in an area to allow them to cover each other.*

Tower Baiting

Thinning out an opponent's army—or a pack of Wolves—is not difficult with this technique. After you

construct several towers, dispatch one of your fastest units—the War Wagon is good—to lure enemy troops to the towers. Your goal is to take down as many of your opponents' units as possible without them catching you. Run loops around the towers if you must. After several laps, your guy will be the last unit standing. (See Figure 3-6.)

Choke Point Defense

Place towers in strategic points, locations where you expect opponents to sift into your kingdom. Such strategic points include gates, wall openings, gaping holes in a forest, and marshes. Towers weaken enemy troops as they enter these choke points, which enables your fresh soldiers to finish them off with more ease. Mangonels are also excellent choke point defense aids.

Figure 3-6   *Lure the enemy through the towers. While the opposition is busy chasing your decoy, your Towers will assault them with spears and arrows.*

Siege Equipment Protection

Mangonels and Onagers pack quite a punch; however, they have a hard time making it through battle. Defending them is imperative unless you have Wood and Gold to burn. Boxing War Wagons around these siege weapons works well most of the time. (See Figure 3-7.) The durability and range of the Wagons buys them more time against attacking enemy infantry and cavalry units. Having a separate cavalry group designed to support your Wagon/Mangonel group is also a good idea.

Figure 3-7   *Box War Wagons around your siege weapons to protect them from enemy attacks.*

Ground Attacks

A weak cast of Stable and Barracks units hampers the Koreans' land-based assaults. However, the War Wagons compensate for these units' lackluster performances. Place them behind melee infantry units that are attacking other archers, enemy cavalry, infantry, or siege units. Their durability and speed enable you to make hit-and-run attacks as well as rushes. War Wagons, in particular, are effective against Persian War Elephants.

Dock Defenses

Defending your Docks from enemy attacks is important for maintaining a maritime presence. Without these structures, your Fishing Ships cannot unload their catch, nor can you create vessels necessary for naval combat. Although many

use Demolition Ships, Galleons, and Trebuchets for this purpose, you have another option—the infamous Turtle Ship. Although slow, its range and Hit Points often vex attackers. Even a Heavy Demolition Ship—the vessel with the most potent attack—takes away less than half of the Elite Turtle Ship's original Hit Points. Place at least one Turtle Ship at each of your Docks, as shown in Figure 3-8, as a protective measure.

Dock Attacks

Turtle Ships are the ultimate all-purpose naval vessel. Great for defending your own Docks, they're also an excellent weapon for taking out enemy Docks. These Ships are highly durable, but they also dish out more attack points than the Elite Cannon Galleon. The only problem is their average range. Solve this by attacking all of an opponent's Docks at one time, sprinkling in some Galleons for back-up. Your

Figure 3-8   *Turtle Ships, with their Hit Points and Armor, are excellent vessels for guarding your Docks.*

opponent's confusion mounts as his or her Docks crumble into the sea. Be sure to protect your Docks, though, while doing this. Otherwise, your opponent might use the same tactic.

Naval Assaults

Your naval assaults are limited because of the Koreans' lack of Demolition Ships and Elite Cannon Galleons, a noticeable problem against civilizations with such units (the Byzantines, Persians, Saracens, Turks, and Vikings). However, you can counter by mixing the Turtle Ship in formations with other vessels. For example, a group of two Turtle Ships (front line) and a Cannon Galleon make an effective combination. Utilized with another group of quicker vessels (two or more Fast Fire Ships), it's possible to take out a threesome of Elite Cannon Galleons. For maximum effect, use the Fast Fire Ships to attack the enemy vessels from behind.

Destroying Siege Weapons

The Koreans are one of the civilizations that have access to the Petard. Churn out a couple of these fellows at your Castle. Place them in towers outside of your village. When an enemy siege weapon rolls by, dispatch a pair of Petards to destroy the unit. Two of these guys can demolish a Heavy Scorpion and Mangonel in one attack.

These tactics concentrate on the military strengths of the Koreans, although the goals are applicable to all civilizations. You probably noticed that this kingdom is well-equipped for battles on both land and sea. With few shortcomings, two unique units, and strong defensive capabilities, the Koreans are suited for a variety of game types and maps.

Chapter Four

THE MAYANS: BACKGROUND, STRATEGY, AND TACTICS

The Mayans lived in the lower part of Mesoamerica and occupied the Yucatán Peninsula and the Petén region (modern Honduras and Guatemala). Scholars have traced the civilization's origins back to the Olmec culture, circa 2000 BCE. Although settling on rough terrain—full of mountains, jungles, and coastlines— the Mayans survived by adopting a strong agricultural-based lifestyle. Maize, cacao, and tropical fruits were some of their most popular crops. Existing in independent city-states, the Mayans were similar to the ancient Greeks in that they shared a common culture but were not unified politically. The Mayan civilization's religion and government, of course, centered on its farming economy.

The Mayapán Empire (the origin of the word "Mayan") existed for over a thousand years before a series of calamities destroyed the civilization. Strongest from 600 to 900 CE, the Empire began crumbling in the tenth century. Internal conflicts between the city-states, natural disasters, and diseases from the New World took their toll. Archeologists have sorted out a great deal of information about these peoples from Mayan artifacts and hieroglyphics and have examined the civilization's evolving political system, its religious beliefs, and, of course, its notorious penchant for human sacrifice. Scholars are still excavating sites and analyzing relics to learn more.

We do, however, know quite a bit about the Mayans, who were at times barbaric and also sophisticated. Their proficiency in mathematics and astronomy amazed Old World settlers. The Mayans constructed elaborate calendars based on the planets' positions. They also used zero in their arithmetic operations, a feature the Europeans later adopted. Their architectural monuments—sturdy and impressive—are as famous as those of the Egyptians and Aztecs. The large, terraced pyramid remnants and smaller plazas—many still standing today—are a reminder of this civilization's great place in the New World's history.

Mayan Attributes

The Mayans are an archer civilization. Many of their attributes, including their unique unit, involve archery. Some of the other special features they offer are improvements in areas (such as defenses), Eagle Warrior strength, and resource use. Take heed, however: The Mayans are one of the most difficult civilizations to command because they lack cavalry and gunpowder-based units. Other than the foot Archers, infantry, and Monks, the civilization has few strengths. To stay on top of things, it's essential that you know how to use these attributes to your advantage.

Unique Unit: Plumed Archer

The Plumed Archer arrives on the scene as soon as you erect a Castle. An upgrade, of course, is possible in the Imperial Age. The Elite Plumed Archer is quick on his feet and has a range equal to the Arbalest, the Britons' Longbowman, and the Koreans' War Wagon. The regular Plumed Archer is quick but has less range than the Elite Plumed Archer and the same firing distance as an ordinary Archer, the Mongols' Elite Mangudai, and the Chinese's Elite Chu Ko Nu.

Unfortunately, despite their speed and range, the Plumed Archers have one of the weakest attacks among mobile land units. Their Hit Points are high but not nearly as impressive as those of the Korean War Wagons. In typical combat situations, use these guys in line formations with Eagle Warriors and Two-Handed Swordsmen. (See Figure 4-1.)

Figure 4-1   *Escort Plumed Archers behind Eagle Warriors when going into battle.*

Unique Technology: El Dorado

El Dorado increases the Eagle Warrior's Hit Points. Researched at the Castle, this technology almost doubles the unit's strength. In fact, after you implement it, Eagle Warriors have the second highest number of Hit Points of any infantry unit in *Microsoft Age of Empires II*. Only the Elite Teutonic Knight has more. However, unlike the Teutons' unique unit, the Eagle Warrior is quicker and requires fewer resources for training (but his attack is much weaker). Along with the Plumed Archer, the Eagle Warrior will become a large part of your military strategy.

Team Bonus: Walls Cost –50 Percent

At first, this attribute might not appear to be of much assistance because walls require few resources anyway. However, with the Mayans, you need to construct more of these structures than usual because of your lack of cavalry and gunpowder-related units. You'll be surprised in the long run how much Stone you save, which allows you to construct Towers, Wonders, and Castles with more ease in the Castle and Imperial Ages. The longer lasting resources attribute offers you further assistance in these endeavors by providing you with more materials for building other units and structures.

Start with Eagle Warrior, +1 Villager, and –50 Food

The Mayans are one of only three civilizations that begin games with a different population configuration. (The Aztecs and Chinese are the other two, whereas only the Persians start games with a different resource configuration.) Because horses were not indigenous to the Americas, Mayans and Aztecs do not have mounted units. Thus, instead of a Scout Cavalry, Mayan players start play with an Eagle Warrior. This is an advantage because Eagle Warriors have slightly more Hit Points, Attack Points, and speed than the Scout Cavalry does. Use the Eagle Warrior to get the upper hand on land exploration.

> **Tip:** *Except when playing against the Aztecs—who begin with an Eagle Warrior, too—you have the fastest and most powerful unit in the Dark Age. Use your Eagle Warrior to harass opponents; wound Villagers; and slay their Deer, Wild Turkeys, and Sheep. The later tactic spoils enemy food supplies, preventing opponents from getting the most of their resources. The enemy Scout Cavalry will try to stop you, but the Eagle Warrior has enough speed to escape. Doing this drives opponents crazy by keeping their economy behind the times.*

Although you begin with –50 Food, the additional Villager can help in the opening seconds by claiming more Sheep or Wild Turkeys than your counterparts.

Resources Last 20 Percent Longer

Mayans have an efficient economy. Their Food, Wood, Stone, and Gold resources last 20 percent longer than those for other civilizations. This attribute is beneficial for churning out more units and defenses than average; increased

efficiency at wall-building and Archery Range production aid you further. Because the Mayans aren't an offensive power-house—winning by Conquest is rather difficult for the inexperienced—this feature is helpful for Wonder-related and Relic-related victories. A strong economy is a critical element in a successful defense and allows you to focus on creating reinforcements instead of reseeding Farms. (See Figure 4-2.)

Figure 4-2 *An efficient economy enables the Mayans to erect more defenses, which makes protecting their Wonder a lot easier.*

Archery Range Unit Costs Decrease in Feudal, Castle, and Imperial Ages

As the Mayans proceed through the Ages, their Archery Ranges produce units more efficiently. In the Feudal Age, Archery Range units cost 10 percent less. This decreases to 20 percent less during the Castle Age. By the Imperial Age, Archery Range units cost 30 percent less. Although you cannot apply this feature when building Plumed Archers (they're created at the Castle), it is important when you produce Skirmishers, Archers, Crossbowmen, and Arbalests. Furthermore, because Mayans do not have access to Cavalry Archers and Hand Cannoneers, the ability to churn out more Archery Range units than usual is a boon.

Mayan Strategies

Cunning and experience are often necessary when you play as the Mayans. The civilization has only a few strengths. Overall, though, weaknesses and mediocrity in a number of areas plague the Mayans. The Mayans lack cavalry and gunpowder-related units, and the highest tier Barracks, Archery Range, and Dock units are not available. This is a serious drawback in the final stages of the game, especially when you realize that gunpowder units hamper the Mayans from building the highest tier Tower (the Bombard Tower) and the absence of Stables prevent the Mayans from using the Paladin. Furthermore, the only available Imperial Age Siege Workshop is the Siege Ram. (See Figure 4-3.)

With such shortcomings, the Mayans rank with the Aztecs, Goths, and Vikings as the most difficult civilizations in the hands of *Age of Empires II* novices.

The Mayans have several strengths, but few are of the over-the-top variety. In other words, if you're looking for brute power, the Mayans are not for you. Their lack of gunpowder technology and cavalry units strains newcomers. For instance, the Mayans have an archery civilization, but their lack of cav-

Figure 4-3 *Limitations in areas such as siege weaponry make conquering opponents difficult.*

alry archers and the Hand Cannoneer hinder you in the Imperial Age. The Mayans sport a relatively strong navy. The only problem is that you encounter deficiencies in—you guessed it—the Imperial Age due to the lack of gunpowder technology. This poses serious problems when you battle the naval powerhouses, such as the Byzantines, Japanese, Persians, Saracens, and Vikings.

Tip: *Whereas the Mayans have a superior navy to that of the Aztecs, Montezuma's civilization has stronger infantry units as well as Monks and siege weapons. For the Mayans, playing on water-based maps is best when taking on the Aztecs. When stuck on 80–100 percent land-filled maps, use El Dorado to give your Eagle Warriors the edge over the Aztec's Eagle Warriors.*

Note: *The Mayans are best for playing game types such as Wonder Race and Defend the Wonder. They are not ideal for Random Map Conquests or Death Match scenarios.*

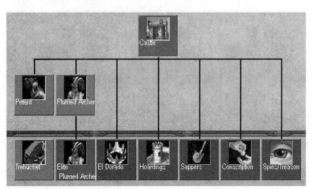

Figure 4-4   *Mayan Castles can create all Castle-related units and all but one technology.*

Victory usually depends upon your infantry, Castle technology and units, and powerful Monks. The Mayan's strongest military feature lies in its arsenal of infantry units. They have access to all units except the Champion. Furthermore, the Blacksmith's Mail Armor (Scale, Chain, and Plate) makes these soldiers more durable. Castles are a necessity for the Mayans. You can construct Plumed Archers and Trebuchets there, as well as Petards. All Castle technologies are available except Anarchy (as shown in Figure 4-4). Monks are also quite useful because they have access to all religious powers except two, Redemption and Illumination. Use these strengths together to win Relic-based and Wonder-based contests.

Mayan Tactics

Unlike the Koreans, the Mayans are not an easy civilization to handle. Handling them requires some subtle tactics. Conquering opponents is difficult. Pursue this in the early stages of the game before heavy hitters such as the Bombard Tower, Cannon Galleon, and Heavy Camel enter the scene. For the most part, your Monks play an integral part in all game types. Also, your infantry and archery units, including the

Eagle Warriors and Plumed Archers, are important for combat. Following are a few tactics you should use when you play as the Mayans.

Marauder Tactics

The Eagle Warrior, due to his speed, is an excellent unit for hit-and-run attacks. Dispatch a group of these guys to chip away at the opponent's economy. Focus on an enemy kingdom's peripheral sites, such as Lumber Camps, Mining Camps, Mills, Houses, and Towers. Raze these structures, and slay any Villagers roaming the area. (See Figure 4-5.) Combine Plumed Archers, Elite Skirmishers, and Crossbowmen to mount successful rushes.

Relic Gathering

When you play as the Mayans, you have a difficult time destroying all of an opponent's units and structures. The civilization has some of the strongest Monks in the game, so try for a Relic victory. First concentrate on building defenses in the Dark and Feudal Ages. Focus on erecting Walls and Towers

Figure 4-5 *Eagle Warriors burn down a Korean Barracks.*

around your village. Create a Monastery in the Castle Age. Produce several Monks, and place them in a Box formation with Eagle Warriors and Plumed

Archers. (See Figure 4-6.) Next send these parties out to locate Relics. To improve your Monks' speed and Hit Points, research Fervor and Sanctity.

Figure 4-6 *Use the Box formation to protect your Monks.*

Garrison Attacks

Although most people garrison units inside structures to protect them from enemy fire, garrisoning is also a nice attack tactic—whether for defensive or offensive purposes. Place several Archers and Plumed Archers in your towers. This tactic usually increases the structure's attack strength. You need the support while you defend a Relic-filled Monastery or Wonder from enemy attacks. String towers from your settlement to your opponent's settlement to use this tactic as an effective offensive strategy.

Improving Ballistics

The Mayans lack gunpowder technology, so you need to do whatever you can to compensate for this loss. Strengthen your Archers with Blacksmith technologies during each Age: Fletching and Padded Archer Armor in the Feudal Age, Bodkin Arrow and Leather Archer Armor in the Castle Age, and Bracer and Ring Archer Armor in the Imperial Age. Thumb Ring technology at the Archery Range improves Archers' range. Research Ballistics, Heat Shot, and Chemistry at the University for additional help in the ballistics department.

Siege Counters

Nothing destroys enemy siege weapons like a cavalry horde. Unfortunately, the Mayans do not have mounted units. Your best bets are your Eagle Warrior and strong infantry. Garrison these guys in some towers. Because your opponents won't see these units, you can surprise them with a sneak attack. When an enemy siege weapon rolls by, dispatch these units from the Tower. Hack the passing Ram, Onager, or Scorpion to splinters.

Holy Healing

The Red Cross didn't exist during Mayan times, but Monks with miraculous powers did. (See Figure 4-7.) When going to war, you'll undoubtedly have casualties. Reduce these with aid from your Monks. First, place your troops in groups. Organize one of the groups with several Monks boxed in by infantry. Now go to war. Leave the Monk group some distance from the enemy settlement (perhaps in one of your Towers), and send your other groups into battle. During the fighting, cycle your wounded groups to the Monks for healing. After the Monks heal 100 percent of your troops, dispatch those troops

Figure 4-7   *The Monk works some of his miracles on the battlefield.*

into battle again. This tactic is great for offensive fronts and enables you to save oodles of time and resources, which are lost when creating new units. Research Herbal Medicine and garrison wounded soldiers in towers to promote faster healing.

Whereas a Monk can heal one unit at a time, multiple units garrisoned in a structure are healed simultaneously.

Converting the Enemy

The Monks are a critical part of most Mayan strategies. Besides healing wounded troops and collecting Relics, Monks can also convert enemy units. This is a rather important tactic for a civilization that lacks cavalry and gunpowder-based units. Use infantry to defend your Cleric, and convert cavalry units so that you can use them yourself. Unfortunately, Mayan monasteries cannot research Redemption, a feature that allows Monks to convert most buildings.

The Mayan civilization is not an easy civilization. It does not win battles with over-the-top brute force—unless it confronts the Aztecs on a map with lots of rivers and/or seas, a location where Mayan naval superiority is obvious. An in-depth strategy is almost always essential, which makes the Mayans far more appealing to experienced *Age of Empires II* gamers than to beginners.

Chapter Five

THE SPANISH: BACKGROUND, STRATEGY, AND TACTICS

During the period in which *Microsoft Age of Empires II: The Conquerors Expansion* takes place, there were three main domains in Spain: two northern Christian kingdoms and a Moorish (Muslim) kingdom in the southern portion. Fighting occurred between all of these kingdoms at one time or another. Eventually, the Christians gained a foothold that would help them drive the Moors out of Spain entirely, and that foothold came in 1469 when Isabel I married Fernando II, uniting the two Christian kingdoms. Granada, the last Moorish stronghold, fell to the Christian forces of Aragon and Castile in 1492.

1492 also ushered in a new era for Spain when Christopher Columbus sailed across the Atlantic Ocean and found the West Indies, thus opening up an entirely new era in Spanish conquests. Within a hundred years, the Aztec civilization was decimated and pillaged by the Spanish Conquistadors. Disease, technology, and some odd circumstances helped the Spanish conquer the Americas despite their numerical disadvantage.

Spanish Attributes

The Spanish are not technologically challenged—indeed they have mastered gunpowder and have some distinct advantages with their ships and special units. Using a combination of standard units and the unique Spanish units, you can overcome any enemy battle or siege situation.

Unique Unit: Conquistador

The Conquistador—upgradeable to the Elite Conquistador—is a very fast and powerful unit that acts as a Hand Cannoneer on a Horse. When in groups, the Conquistadors have an impressive ability to take down enemy units (at a range of six) from afar. Their weapons are powerful and not only do substantial damage but also have a pierce factor that makes them even more potent. Conquistadors are best used to move in quickly, fire their weapons to do the job, and then move away quickly to avoid retribution.

Unique Unit: Missionary

The Missionary is basically a Monk who's mounted on a Horse. Although the Missionary cannot pick up Relics and has a slightly shorter range than a Monk, he costs the same (100 Gold) and can otherwise do everything a Monk can do. The added bonus for a Missionary is that he's on horseback and can move faster than many enemies on foot, making him an excellent weapon for converting slow enemy units.

Unique Technology: Supremacy (Villagers Better in Combat)

This technology might seem like it's not a worthwhile skill to develop, but having the ability to defend an unprotected town center from a surprise attack with just your Villagers will give you an extra layer of comfort in particularly close battles in which every single military unit you have is needed at the front lines.

Team Bonus: Trade Units Generate +33 Percent Gold

Obviously, having this extra Gold might be all that's needed to make the difference between winning and losing in a tight game. As games wear on, Gold becomes an incredibly valuable resource both for upgrades and for many of the higher level units (and anything Monk-related). Building Trade Cogs is a good idea—if you have a Dock—so that you can fully benefit from this team bonus.

Builders Work 30 Percent Faster

This civilization bonus is huge. All things being equal, a Spanish civilization should be able to out-muscle any other civilization based on this characteristic alone. Being able to build structures (and repair them) 30 percent faster means that your Villagers will have more time to harvest Stone, Gold, Wood, and

Food rather than building and that the structures themselves will become functional much faster.

Blacksmith Upgrades Don't Cost Gold

This benefit is somewhat more limited, but it still frees up extra Gold that would otherwise be used in upgrading the critical attributes that the Blacksmith is responsible for. This extra Gold can be used in the Monastery to build up the Monk's and Missionary's skills.

Cannon Galleons Benefit from Ballistics (Firing Faster and More Accurately)

Another huge bonus. When scuffling in a large sea battle where many ships are moving around and supremacy of the seas is at stake, faster, more accurate shots are critical and can often turn the tide of the battle. This benefit is also a great boon to patrol ships that shoot at enemy Trade Cogs, War Ships, or Fishing Vessels because the improved accuracy of the shot can often mean a kill when the enemy might otherwise have escaped.

Spanish Strategies

As the commander of the Spanish forces, you'll need to take advantage of some of this civilization's unique abilities, specifically the ability to generate more Gold from Trade units and to upgrade in the Blacksmith with no Gold cost. You need to channel this extra revenue to areas where you can gain an advantage on your enemy; the area that relies most heavily on Gold is the Monastery. By building up the technology (tech) tree in the Monasteries, you can gain the upper hand by converting enemy buildings and units to the Spanish side.

The Spanish also have unique abilities with their Missionaries—see Figure 5-1—and their Galleons, Cannon Galleons, and Heavy Galleons with their ability to take advantage of research in Ballistics. Also, the Conquistadors, on horseback with their mounted Hand Cannons, are a powerful weapon to use for hit-and-run attacks and for moving quickly to save friendly units that are being overwhelmed by the enemy.

AGE *of* EMPIRES II

Figure 5-1 *The Missionaries are highly mobile and fully functional Monks.*

To be successful as the Spanish, you'll need to upgrade your ships to the top of the technology tree and invest in groups of Conquistadors. Because your builders work 30 percent faster and you have some benefits regarding Gold consumption/acquisition, you can often get a technological and Town Center jump on your rivals (especially when starting off on equal footing).

Spanish Tactics

Spanish tactics are all about speed, power, and upgrading the navy, but there are also several specific tactics that will make your life easier when you're trying to emerge victorious as a Spanish warrior-King.

Resource Management

Build quickly. Don't waste any time at all because your civilization has a bonus that enables your troops to build 30 percent faster. If you don't take advantage of this and get off to a quick start, the bonus will be largely negated. As mentioned before, you have some Gold-related bonuses, so use your extra Gold to develop your Monastery's technology tree.

Unit Management

Keep your units grouped together by kind, with a few stray Knights or Scouts on horseback to patrol the perimeter of your city. The key to all units is preventing them from going off and doing something you don't want them to. Avoid unnecessary conflicts where your troops get lured away from safety.

Defense

Spanish walls work as well as any walls, but because you have a building bonus, you can build and repair your walls and gates 30 percent faster, making the defense of your city somewhat easier if you have some Villagers around to do the work. Guard Towers are always a good idea when defending your city. When it comes to defending in the open field, put your Conquistadors in the back and your melee units up front—this will at least protect the mounted Conquistadors from hand-to-hand combat and will give them a chance to run if the battle's being lost.

Reconnaissance

Scouts are always good for reconnaissance because they're cheap and fast, but you must also consider the Conquistador—see Figure 5-2—with his powerful ranged attack, and the Missionary, who not only moves reasonably fast but converts stray enemy units as well.

Figure 5-2 *The Conquistador is excellent as a scout, as well as a lure to coax enemy units to follow him.*

The Decoy

A Conquistador is a great decoy—the enemy will almost always chase down this unit because it's an offensive unit. The Conquistador, however, is deceptively fast and can pull enemy units out of position or act as a decoy that will distract the enemy while you attack elsewhere.

The Lure

In naval battles, use a Galleon or a Fishing Boat as a lure while your more powerful ships lie in wait. Your Galleon's ability to fire more accurately and faster will crush any enemy ships that you trap.

Ships

Build your naval technology tree up as fast as you can because your ships will benefit from Ballistics research (in the Archery Range). This means that your ships fire both faster and more accurately, so for the Spanish a large navy can easily make the difference between victory and defeat. If your enemy occupies even a small amount of coast, your ships will be able to overpower him or her to gain the beachhead for landing your Transports.

Combined Arms

Put Swordsmen, Conquistadors, a few Monks (or Missionaries), and a group of Knights together and you'll have a powerful nonsiege group that you can take into battle and emerge victorious with. The Conquistadors can be moved around to any point in the battlefield where their Hand Cannons can benefit you while the melee units fight it out.

PART II

The Conquerors: Walkthroughs and Strategies

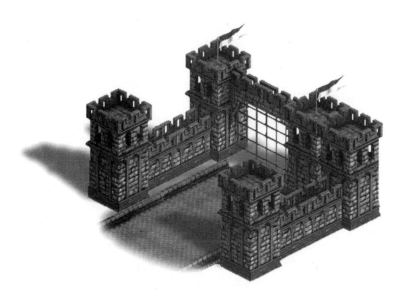

Chapter Six

THE MONTEZUMA CAMPAIGN

Reigning over the vast Aztec empire and the sacred city of Tenochtitlan, Montezuma II was confused and conflicted by the landing of strange men on the Mexican coast. Arriving on April 21, 1519, Cortez happened to give the appearance of fulfilling an Aztec prophecy. On that date—9 Wind Day in the Aztec calendar—the god Quetzacoatl was to return by sea from the East, with light skin, a dark beard, and black robes. Cortez seemed to fit the prophecy, but were he and his men gods to worship or mere men? Montezuma's uncertainty emboldened the aggressive Spaniard, who wanted the enormous wealth of the Aztec nation. Taking advantage of Montezuma's hesitancy, Cortez and the Spaniards sought to control the Aztecs through their leader.

In the Montezuma Campaign, you'll witness the tribal discord under Montezuma's rule, which is a prelude to the appearance of Cortez and his army. Beginning as a commander under Montezuma, you'll come to lead in your own right and turn back the Spanish threat to your sacred city of Tenochtitlan.

Mission One: Reign of Blood

Objectives:

- Capture the four Shrines (Monasteries) sacred to Quetzalcoatl.
- Place a sacred Relic in each of the four Shrines.

Hints:

- You must defend the Shrines sacred to the god Quetzalcoatl. Making new Monasteries will not be sufficient to please him.
- Your enemies will attempt to destroy the Shrines to embarrass you before the gods. Therefore, do not attempt to claim the Shrines until you can defend them.
- Aztec Priests (Monks) are very powerful when fully upgraded. After you capture a Shrine and advance to the Castle Age, you can train Monks.
- The Aztecs are restricted to the Castle Age.

Scout Reports:

- Montezuma's forces (green) begin in the Feudal Age with only a few soldiers. These few must defend the Aztec town from early attacks.
- You have three enemies: the Tlatiluco (red), the Tepanaca (orange), and the Xochimilco (purple). The Tlatiluco are located to the west. You can deal with their army of swordsmen and Eagle Warriors relatively early.
- The Tepanaca dwell to the north of your town. Their walls may keep you out of their town until you have siege weapons. They train Archers and Eagle Warriors.

Tip: *The Xochimilco are your most dangerous enemy. They live far to the north and train Archers and Scorpions. Do not engage them until you have many Eagle Warriors at your command.*

Note: *Your Aztec units are green, which also happens to be the color of the surrounding forest! Get used to using the Idle Villager button and Idle Unit key (the comma) to help spot lost and laggardly assets.*

First Walkthrough: The Outer Path

Your objective is to get to four Shrines and put the relics you find at each Shrine inside. You won't be able to build Monks before you reach the first Shrine, and after you reveal a Shrine you'll be obligated to defend it.

First send your Eagle Warriors to scout nearby while you build more Villagers to get your economy going. Concentrate on Food and Wood early, although soon enough you'll be turning toward Gold in a big way. While scouting, note the multiple Gold deposits to the west and the single deposit to the north, which is the one you should mine first. If you run across any Turkeys, send them to your Town Center.

You'll face a number of early patrols and attacks by enemy Aztec and Mayan forces alike. Because the Mayans are good with the bow—particularly those from Tepanaca, to the north—make sure you have plenty of Skirmishers early to deal with their threat. Regular infantry units are also important, however, so don't neglect a general buildup of arms or your upgrades at the Blacksmith.

Tip: *The local Jaguars (the furry animals) are aggressive and attack in groups. Although a single Jaguar isn't too much of a threat even to a Villager, a group of Jaguars can do real damage. If attacks occur near your Town Center, garrison all Villagers and then target the Jaguars with the Town Center. You must target manually because Jaguars are not considered enemies.*

Stay on the defensive, and mine Stone near your Town Center. When you're close to being able to build a Castle, advance to the Castle Age and continue to upgrade your infantry and archery units.

At some point, infantry raiders from Tlatiluco will become an almost steady stream, which is your cue that it's time to build a Castle near your Town Center both to help with defenses and to allow you to build Jaguar Warriors. After you build the Castle, stock it with Skirmishers, but leave a few slots open for healing and garrisoning units.

When you have Gold coming in, and plenty of Food, start cranking out Jaguar Warriors in big bunches. Although you'll want to add Archers and siege weapons down the line, for now a few Skirmishers provide sufficient support. When you have at least ten Jaguar Warriors, send them west to locate the southern Shrine and have a few Villagers start mining the Gold deposits to the west as well.

When you reveal the southern Shrine, build four Monks. Have the first one set the Relic inside and two of the four head to your village to help heal the defensive troops. Augment your ten Jaguar Warriors with some Archers or Skirmishers, and send three or four Rams along to them as well.

While leaving a small defensive force of infantry and ranged weapons at the Shrine, send the Rams and the rest of your troops and Monks against the Aztec village of Tlatiluco. Have them tear down Guard Towers and other buildings; send more forces to join them until the city submits to your rule.

By now you'll be close to your 75-unit maximum, but you should also have a pretty good idea of what number and mix of forces will keep your village safe from attack. As you lose units in battle, replace them with better units and keep at least two Monks with them at all times. Upgrade to Herbal Medicine at your Shrine to help injured units heal faster at your Town Center or Castle, and keep the siege engines coming, along with a Villager or two to keep them in tip-top shape.

> **Tip:** *That central Shrine looks tempting, but don't touch it! The Mayans at Tepanaca have a clear path to it from the north and will destroy it immediately.*

> **Note:** *When the Tlatiluco Town Center falls, more Villagers than you're ever going to want to see pour out and head for the jungle, where they try to set up a new town. Some good ranged infantry can keep you from having to track down all the new buildings they put up, just so you can get a surrender.*

When you swing north, you'll come to a constricted pass in the jungle just to the left of which will be a Xochimilco Siege Workshop and Castle. Tempting as it might be to rush around the corner, don't! Instead, bring your Mangonels and ranged infantry into the pass, and then tempt the waiting enemy units—of which there are a great many from both remaining Mayan towns—to attack.

Remember that you're facing Mayan troops, who are handy with a bow. Protect your Monks and Jaguar Warriors accordingly, and mass your own ranged fire, target by target, while you send your injured units back to heal. After a while, you should stem the tide, at which time you'll be able to push out into what is literally a crossroads

| 2769 | 2320 | 2470 | 4626 | 51/75 | Castle Age |

Castle

3701/4800
11+1 (4)
8+1

Mayans
Xochimilco
Enemy

Ensemble Studios

CONQUERORS

Microsoft

Figure 6-1 *When you finally have control of the pass, your Rams will make short work of the Castle.*

between Xochimilco and Tepanaca to the north. When you can, sneak your Rams around to the left and take out the Castle (as shown in Figure 6-1) along with the Siege Workshop if you didn't already destroy it from the path.

Push west with your forces, and destroy every important building in Xochimilco. If you need replacements, have a Villager build the buildings you need on the spot instead of sending back to your Village for help. Keep the pressure on, and you'll clear most of the town by the time you discover the river west of the city.

To reach the second Shrine, you need to have a Villager build a Dock on the river. Build a Transport Ship, and board two ranged units; then sail them across to the other side. There you'll find a pack of Jaguars waiting to slow your claim, but you should be able to cut a path through them easily. Reveal the Shrine, build a Monk, and place the second Relic inside.

After Xochimilco surrenders, only Tepanaca to the north remains. Swing north with your full force bearing down on the third Shrine, and take it as fast as you can. Press ahead and threaten the city of Tepanaca itself (as shown in Figure 6-2); meet any counter attacks it sends your way. Attack also with most of the troops at your Village to add pressure from the east.

Quickly send a Monk and small escort from your Village to the fourth Shrine in the center of the forest. Have the Monk put the Relic in the Shrine, and the gods will grant you victory.

Second Walkthrough: Stealing Through the Jungle

Begin by ramping up Food, Wood, and Stone production and using your initial Eagle Warriors to scout out the local area. Don't have them travel too far, however, and make sure they're handy when the big cats come after your town folk.

As you build, do *not* use any of your original 200 Gold; keep it in the bank until you build your Castle, when you'll be ready to start mining some of the Gold deposits you'll have discovered. Send your Villagers into the Town Center every time there's trouble and then back to work after you crush the enemy threat.

Upgrade to Town Watch, and build an Archery Range and Blacksmith if you don't already have them. Stockpile food as you go, and advance to the

Figure 6-2   *With three Shrines and Tepanaca under siege, it's time to go for the fourth Shrine!*

Castle Age when you can. Build a Castle close to your Town Center for added defensive fire; then crank out a few more Villagers, and send them off to the Gold mine to the north-northeast. Build houses in advance so that you're free to build to your maximum 75-unit limit.

Upgrade to Squires at the Barracks if you haven't. Spend the Gold you mine only on upgrades at the Blacksmith, on upgrades to Elite Skirmishers at the Archery Range, and on five or so Eagle Warriors, who will show you the way to victory.

The objective is to find paths to the four Shrines *without* actually discovering any of the shrines. This method avoids making the shrines yours, which would make them the object of enemy assaults. All you want to do for now is discover *how* to get to each Shrine when the time comes. The Shrine in the south is easy enough, as is the Shrine in the center. Of particular concern are the Shrines in the north and west, but to scout them out you have to be careful while passing the center Shrine. When you come to a fork, take the left path, and stay to the left (as shown in Figure 6-3), so you don't accidentally reveal the center Shrine.

Unfortunately, your forays to find the least defended paths to the northern and western Shrines are certain suicide missions for many of the Eagle Warriors you send, but getting the right information is critical to gaining access to all four Relics.

Although the northern Shrine looks at hand when you come out of the central path, you need to head northeast, past a pool of Guard Towers and a Town Center,

Figure 6-3 *While passing west of the center Shrine, you might glimpse a Relic, but let that be all you see.*

before you can find the way. Again, don't get close enough to actually discover the Shrine—just make sure you know how to get there later.

The path to the Shrine in the west is much more difficult. First, you need your Eagle Warriors to find a way through the Xochimilco town that doesn't take you past the murderous Town Center and Castle. Second, when you finally do make it through the town, you'll discover that the way to the Shrine is blocked by a river.

However, as you've been running through enemy-held territory, you've seen how the enemy guards fall in behind your Eagle Warriors, in pursuit. The net result of this is that your Eagle Warriors are clearing a path for other units to follow in relative safety, and that's going to be the enemy's undoing.

To locate the western Shrine, build a force of Elite Skirmishers, a few Villagers, and some Eagle Warriors. Send the Eagle Warriors slightly ahead of the Skirmishers and Villagers, through the Xochimilco village, toward the north end of the river. Slip the Skirmishers and Villagers in behind the Eagle Warriors, and have the Eagle Warriors turn south as the Skirmishers hold and the Villagers break for the river. (See Figure 6-4.)

Now send the Eagle Warriors and Skirmishers northeast to lure the Xochimilco defenders while the Villagers build a Dock in a flash. Launch a Transport, and then ferry a couple of Eagle Warriors across the river to a landing full of Jaguars. Carve your way through the Jags, and reveal the Shrine.

> **Tip:** *Send a couple of Eagle Warriors to the shrine in the center. There might be a Mayan Plumed Archer lying in wait there.*

Build a Priest, and have him place the Relic inside; then head your remaining units out toward the north. Send two small forces to discover the Shrines in the south and center; get Priests underway at each. Then run the bulk of your forces up to the Shrine in the north.

Time your discovery of the central Shrine so that it is the last, and plan to defend the site for a while until the fourth Priest appears to pick up the last Relic. Place the final Relic in the last Shrine, and the jungle is yours.

Figure 6-4 *Distract the enemy from the river, and then slip your Villagers in to build a Dock.*

Mission Two: The Triple Alliance

Objectives:

- Deliver the summons of war to the Texcoco Town Center.
- Deliver the summons of war to the Tlacopan Town Center.

Hints:

- Use your Eagle Warriors to locate a suitable location for an Aztec town.
- Be aware of Tlaxcalan war ships on streams and rivers.
- The Aztecs have two powerful infantry units: the Jaguar Warrior, which can easily defeat other infantry, and the Eagle Warrior, which is a good counter for Archers, horses, and siege weapons.
- The Aztecs cannot yet advance to the Imperial Age.

Scout Reports:

- Montezuma's forces (green) have only a few Eagle Warriors. These messengers must visit the other two members of the Triple Alliance, the Tlacopan (yellow) and Texcoco (purple).
- The Tlacopan train swordsmen and Eagle Warriors, whereas the Texcoco train archers and Mangonels.
- You'll need all these troops to defeat the wicked Tlaxcala (red), who live to the north across the rivers. The Tlaxcala are known for their Archers, infantry, and Mad Shaman.

First Walkthrough: Sailing Along

You must deliver a summons of war to your two allies in Texcoco and Tlacopan. Send your four Eagle Warriors west through the shallows. Make sure they avoid two Jaguars that might be hot on their tail. When they come to land again, head them northwest until they reach the Tlacopan Town Center.

After the Tlacopan leader begrudgingly agrees to join your cause, send your Eagle Warriors east-northeast through more shallows and then across a road to the shore of a river. Follow the riverside north until you find shallows that allow you to cross to the opposite bank.

Note: *You might learn that there is a Shrine nearby and that bringing ten Jaguar Warriors there will net you a reward. Quell your curiosity, and stick to the task at hand; the Shrine is guarded by enemy Watch Towers, and you don't have time to fool with them.*

Head east, crossing overland until you reach the Texcoco Town Center. There again the local leader begrudgingly acknowledges Montezuma's orders to join his forces in war, at which time you'll be told your mission: destroy the four Town Centers belonging to the Tlaxcalan enemy, whose city lies in the west.

Note: *Don't build your Town Center until you're sure it's where you want it. You can build only one until you get to the Castle Age, so don't be hasty.*

A transport will arrive from Montezuma carrying four Villagers, sailing up the river to set up your forward base. Stop the ship at the first shallows on the eastern side of the river, where you'll find a small inlet. Let the Villagers out, and send them east-northeast to look for a clearing with Forage Bushes and a large Gold deposit nearby. When they find it, build your Town Center there and send your original Eagle Warriors to scout out the eastern corner of your territory looking for resources.

Start piling on the resources, basic buildings, and upgrades, and plan on keeping it up until the very end. Gold is particularly important, so locate it and begin mining it. Build a dock in the inlet by your Village, and when you have enough Stone, build a Castle nearby as well. Although you're in the rear area, and your allies will take most of the abuse, don't neglect your defenses in case there are surprise attacks.

Advance to the Castle Age as soon as possible; then upgrade to War Galleys at the Dock. Add a Shrine and a Priest or two, but don't build too many defensive units just yet. Instead, start launching War Galleys and Fire Ships by the tens, massing them on the river outside your inlet. Upgrade to Careening when you can, and build two transports as well. If you don't have a Siege Workshop, build it too.

Sail your first ten or so ships north until they enter the shallows where two rivers converge. Set your Armada to a defensive stance, and leave the ships there to take care of any enemy vessels or units trying to pass by. Keep building more ships, and anchor them with the others in the shallows until you have a blockade of twenty-five vessels or more.

Pick ten War Galleys and ten Fire Ships and send them west, sweeping upstream. Take out any enemy War Galleys you come across, but don't delay too long to fight isolated units onshore. At your inlet, stock two Villagers and three Rams each in your Transport Ships; then send them up the river behind your Armada. If your ships start to get chewed up, let some of the Villagers off onshore to repair the damaged boats.

When you come to the first fork in the river, take the left channel west and follow it to the end. You'll find two Docks there—which you should sink, as shown in Figure 6-5— and a Town Center. When the Docks are gone and the river safe, bring your Transports

> **Tip:** *At the shallows you've blockaded, you'll see your Allies attacking toward the west. Give them a hand if they come running by with the enemy hot on their tails.*

Figure 6-5   *Destroy those Docks and you'll cut the enemy's shipping capacity by two thirds!*

up and have three Rams knock down the Town Center. When they're through and you've made repairs, send three Rams straight north and the other three east across the small peninsula you just sailed around. You should find the second and third Town Centers on those bearings, and you should be able to destroy them with relative ease.

Recover your Rams and sail back to the main channel, turning to port (left) and sailing northwest. Keep a wary eye out for enemy Priests onshore, and don't stop until you come to the next Dock. Destroy the Dock, and then follow the river north, taking the branch toward the east. If you've lost any vessels, make more, but send them only as far as the blockade.

Have your Armada follow the river until you spot the last Town Center on a small hill on the northern bank. Send ships around to the east side where they can fire on the building; bring up a Transport, and have the Rams hit the Town Center hard. In moments it should fall, taking Tlaxcala with it. Within the next moment, your allies will turn on you.

Quickly send your Armada—transports and all—back to the shallows just north of Tlacopan. Meanwhile, at your Village, begin building Mangonels, Crossbowmen, Elite Skirmishers, and Eagle Warriors, and use them to hold your city against the coming tide of Plumed Archers from neighboring Texcoco. Send your Armada of War Galleys and Fire Ships south against the northwest shore of Tlacopan. Shell and burn every major building you can, and when those are gone send your Rams against the Town Center, which should be visible. When your Rams start their attack, send at least half of your fleet around to the city's southeastern shore and have them do as much damage there as they can.

Texcoco will be putting pressure on your city, so use any ships you lose as a chance to recover ground forces for the defense of your town. Your eventual objective will be the Texcoco Castle to your northwest, but it's almost impossible to get there too early. Do your best to keep from being overrun, and continue upgrading and researching while you stockpile resources.

After a while, your relentless bombardment of Tlacopan will succeed and the city will surrender. Immediately send all surviving vessels, as well as your new ships at the blockade, to the north. Guide them back around to the southeast into the rear area of the Texcoco city and forces, and have them attack the Watch Tower there. Next sail toward the Town Center, attacking any forces and structures along the shore.

Your shore bombardment of the Texcoco village should bring your ground forces the relief they need. Have a force of Petards and upgraded Rams ready to strike, and when the forces of Texcoco fall back to fight your ships, destroy the Castle immediately. Without opposition, you should be able to unleash the full fury of your army on the rest of the city. Crossbowmen and Mangonels can sweep ahead, destroying everything in their path. (See Figure 6-6.) If you have any Villagers in your Transport Ships, build a Siege Workshop in the enemy backfield and add a third point of attack.

When you destroy the last of the Texcoco war machine, victory will be yours, but your relief might be brief. Look north, and you'll see strangers coming from the sea.

Second Walkthrough: To the Swift Go the Spoils

Start by running your Eagle Warriors to their appointed destinations and bringing forth a Transport from Montezuma. Sail the Transport to the first branch on the left, sending it down to the south until you see a Gold deposit on the western bank. Let your Villagers off there, and have them build a Town Center on the other side of the brick-paved path, next to the lagoon. (See Figure 6-7.)

Have your Eagle Warriors in Texcoco scout to the near west to look for a Relic. When they find it, dispatch them north to seek for two more. Return your Eagle Warriors to the first Relic, and leave them there to defend it against Tlaxcalan Priests coming to claim it.

Figure 6-6 *When your Armada distracts the enemy, press your advantage and destroy the town.*

Figure 6-7 *Although the site of your Town Center is a bit cramped, it's also easy to defend.*

When your Town Center is up, build ten more Villagers and put them to work gathering resources and building a bustling city. You have plenty of time to stockpile and build, what with the Tlacopans to your northwest absorbing most of the small assaults that the Tlaxcalans will throw your way. To gain every advantage, do the following:

- Keep your city compact, and leave space in the center to build a Castle.
- Send Villagers to the nearest eastern island to mine Stone and Gold. Set up a Mill for farming, too, but stay away from the far branch of the river.
- Build two Docks: one just upriver from your village and one in the heart of the lagoon. Launch warships from the river Dock to act as a defensive screen by blocking access to your city. Build Fishing Boats at the Dock in the lagoon; then look for the plentiful schools of Shore Fish, as well as larger schools in the river.
- Save space by building a Lumber Camp on the island to upgrade your woodcutting, but gather most of the Wood from around your Town Center. Not only is there more wood to harvest there, but collecting it helps clear space for more buildings.
- Build a Market and several Trade Carts, and trade with the Market at Tlacopan. Don't try to trade with Texcoco; your carts will be waylaid by the Tlaxcalans.
- Build enough houses to max your available units out at 75. To save space, build some of the houses on the island.

Note: *Don't forget to build a Blacksmith and upgrade your infantry and Archer attributes. Just because Garland Wars is out of reach doesn't mean you can't be stronger.*

After you advance to the Castle Age, build a Castle in the center of your city and produce three Petards. Have the Petards head north and blow the Tlaxcalan gate to allow you inside. Run an Eagle Warrior in and up to the Shrine to learn the offer of the Temple of Tlaloc; then get him out before the Tlaxcalan Watch Towers skewer him.

Build ten Jaguar Warriors, and send them to the Shrine only long enough for them to be blessed. Run them out again—taking care that they avoid the 450-hit point Son of Ornlu—and build a few Rams to take out the Watch Towers. Not only are they shooting at your new Shrine, but they're going to be in the way later and you won't have time to deal with them then.

By now your allies should have scouted out the Tlaxcalan territory enough to reveal where the four Town Centers are. Upgrade to Crossbowmen if you haven't; then build a force of five Rams, fifteen Crossbowmen, and two Monks. Load two of your ten 450-hit point Jaguar Warriors in each of the five Rams, and send your whole force west through Tlacopan.

Pass the Tlacopan Town Center, cross the shallows to the west, and then head northwest, staying as clear of the river as possible. When you come to a shallows crossing to the north, take it and cross quickly. If you come under naval bombardment, don't turn back to fight; just keep going north toward the first of the Tlaxcalan Town Centers. After you take out the first Town Center, drive north between the houses and knock down the Castle. Turn west and take out the second Town Center by the river, and then turn north and take out the third—all as quickly as you can.

Turn your column northeast, snaking through the backwaters toward the fourth Town Center, again keeping away from the rivers as much as possible. When you approach the fourth Town Center, lead with your Rams and try to knock it down quickly. Unlike the other sites, here you're going to stir up a real counterattack, which will take a while to die off even after the Tlaxcalans have surrendered. Try to retain as many units as possible because your Allies are suddenly going to turn on you.

When your Allies attack, you'll lose the line-of-sight they scouted. Remembering where the Texcoco Town Center was, send your column of Rams and Archers there to the east, across the rivers. In the south, by your city, send all Villagers to the island to continue mining resources, and shift half of your ships into the lagoon. Create a killing ground for the Tlacopan troops streaming toward your town by cutting them down with fire from your ships, Castle, and Town Center.

Immediately destroy your Trade Carts and Fishing Boats to free up more units, and stock your Castle and Town Center with Archers. Build a few Mangonels, and station them in the shadow of your Castle, where the enemy shouldn't be able to reach them.

When you reach Texcoco, use your Rams to destroy the two Archery Ranges you'll come across on your way to the Town Center, and try to destroy the Town Center next. When your Rams are destroyed and your high hit-point Jaguar Warriors appear, direct them to take out Plumed Archers until they're about half down in damage, and then run them toward the river and a Transport waiting to take them back to your village for healing.

When the initial rush of the Tlacopan dies down, build ten Rams and ten more Jaguar Warriors. Send the Rams around through the Temple of Tlaloc (as shown in Figure 6-8) into the rear of the Tlacopan city, and send the Jaguar Warriors and some

AGE

of

EMPIRES II

Figure 6-8 *Send your Rams through the Temple of Tlaloc, and they'll appear in the Tlacopan rear.*

Crossbowmen in from the lagoon side. Destroy the Town Center and the main buildings; then hunt down the remaining units until the Tlacopan concede defeat.

Build another Transport or two, stock them all with Rams and Crossbowmen, along with Jaguar Warriors and Eagle Warriors and a few Priests, and set sail for Texcoco. Drop half your forces off at the small inlet in the south, and the other half off in the center. Attack the Castle from both directions by sending Rams.

Destroying the Castle should give you free reign to lay waste to Texcoco, but you'll need to keep your troops in line to win out without calling in reinforcements. If you can't find the last few enemy forces, use your Eagle Warriors to search the forest to the east. A number of clearings there might conceal Villagers and buildings.

Mission Three: Quetzalcoatl

Objectives:

- Defeat the Tlaxcalans.

Hints:

- The dense rain forest is home to many Jaguars. Be cautious.
- The Tabasco, your allies, live dangerously close to your enemies. It might be possible to save them, but do not despair if Tabasco is destroyed.
- Do not slay the Spanish beasts if they can be of some use.

Scout Reports:

- The Aztecs of Montezuma (green) have a small fortress to the south. In the center of the area is a large cliff, and north of this is your ally, Tabasco (orange). To the west is the sprawling city of your enemies, the Tlaxcala (red). To the east are the Spanish (blue). Their motives are unknown.
- The Spanish are far more powerful. Defeating their cavalry and swordsmen will require siege weapons as their fortress is protected with cannon.

First Walkthrough: Horsing Around

Begin by exploring to the northwest, north, and northeast. You need to locate all the avenues of access to your town so that you can see the directions your enemies will be coming from. Watch out for Jaguars on the paths, and if you can't sneak by them, build a Skirmisher or two to take care of the problem. Scout for resources as well.

> **Note:** *Archers, Skirmishers, and Eagle Warriors led by Monks comprise the Tlaxcala army. You might succeed at slowing their production by attacking Tlaxcala early.*

At the Town Center, set all of your Villagers to working on the fields they're standing on; then build new Villagers to cut Wood and mine the Stone and Gold nearby. Stone is key because it allows you to build a Castle, which qualifies you for the Imperial Age. Don't neglect its harvest or the defense of your vulnerable miners.

When you've scouted out the northwest trail leading through the jungle and you can see how it connects to the path leading to the large Gold deposit, send Villagers up there under guard to build a Stone Wall to cut off direct Tlaxcalan access to your village. Double-check to make sure there aren't any obscured routes enemy units can use to get by your wall, and then send your Villagers to build another Stone Wall east of the Gold.

Your weak ally in the north will probably be defeated by now, but you'll have gained some valuable reconnaissance, and you might still gain the advantage of the line of sight from an Outpost or two. Build your Castle northeast of your Town Center so that it can fire on enemy troops entering your village from any of the remaining open paths. Stock it with upgraded ranged weapons to add punch, and then advance to the Imperial Age as soon as you have the resources. Stay on the defensive until you do.

> **Note:** *If you haven't discovered them, there are Spanish Galleons on the river to the east, and they'll fire at anything. Given their long range, it's best to stay clear of the river at all times, so build that eastern wall close to your Gold mine.*

Build a Monastery and a couple of Monks if you haven't already, and start building Jaguar Warriors, which are excellent at running down Spanish Bombard Cannons.

Research Herbal Medicine to make your Castle even quicker at healing, and start building a few Trebuchets and other heavier arms.

At some point, it will occur to you that stealing the Spaniards' Horses would surely cripple their ability to wage war. However, to go about such a theft requires more than guile, so keep amassing resources and building strong arms.

The first real objective is to build a Dock and take control of the river. The logical place to do so is on the small tributary leading to the pond just north of your town, but you will first need to use Eagle Warriors and other units to distract the nearby Spanish sentries and ships. In any case, do whatever it takes to get a Villager in to build that Dock, and then crank out Fire Ships to take on the Spanish Galleons.

Tip: *You're going to want to build a Dock in the pond. It's a great idea, but you can't actually sail out of the pond, so don't do it! Also, when you build your Dock, you might block the whole stream, so set your gather point to the north.*

On your tours up and down the main river channel, along and through the Spanish territories, notice several things. First, the river does not empty into the sea, meaning the Spanish Galleons there can avoid your fiery wrath. Secondly, the Spanish have regularly spaced guards at their borders, making it difficult to sneak in and out. Finally, a large corral of horses is located right on the riverfront begging you to rustle them.

To gather your first herd, make sure the short river north to the main channel and the parallel road are both clear of enemy units. You're going to want the first Horses you free to have a safe run home without running into Spanish arms.

Note: *When the Horses become "yours," the Spanish troops will fire on them immediately. Do not "adopt" the Horses until you have a hole in the fence that they can escape through, or they will all be killed before you can get them out.*

When the way home is clear, send at least five Fire Ships to the Palisade holding the horses, and have them cut away the southernmost corner and southwestern side. (See Figure 6-9.) Act quickly because Bombard Cannon are headed your way!

When the corral is open, cause the Horses to become yours by sailing a Fire Ship into the **V** of the fencing. Immediately send the Horses south to your corral as you pull your ships back to the tributary that leads toward your town.

When the horses arrive in your corral, give a quick headcount; then gather the bulk of your forces—including Trebuchets—and head northeast along the far eastern path. When you're close to the Spanish Wall and gate, you'll see a tower or two beyond that you should target with your Trebuchets. (See Figure 6-10.)

Fight off any counterattacking units until the towers fall, and then shell the gate until you destroy it. Pack up your Trebuchets, and move into the Spanish rear to shell the Siege Workshop you see opposite a small strip of forest.

Pack up again and move northeast, looking for two corrals standing side by side with a couple of houses in between. When you spot them, unpack your Trebuchets and shell the Palisades until they're open enough for the Horses to escape without becoming jammed in a small gap. Wait for a lull in any fighting, and run one Eagle Warrior into each corral to take possession of the Horses and send them home.

Figure 6-9   *As quickly as you can, burn through the Palisade Wall and the Horses will be yours.*

Now get your Fire Ships back out in the main channel, this time heading east. Send your Trebuchets heading north by slipping them between a Castle on the left and a Bombard Tower on the right. Across the river, you'll find the fourth corral, which you can reach through the shallows, but be ready for attacking Spanish defenders.

Figure 6-10   *Take your time and move deftly in the Spanish rear, and you may escape notice.*

Approach the last corral only as closely as you need to in order to blow a hole in the Palisade, and then send one unit in to get the Horses. Send them home to the corral; then pack up and get out the way you came in. When you have 20 horses in your corral, Cortez will see the folly of a continued fight and withdraw from the battle field.

To deal with the Tlaxcalans, you need only gather resources and field an army of good ranged and infantry units along with a few Mangonels for area coverage. Build a gate in the barrier wall you erected, pour through, and pound away until you finish off the Tlaxcalans. Without Spanish support—or any hope of it—they will quickly fall.

Second Walkthrough: Going for the Gold

While depriving the Spanish of their beasts drives them from the field of battle, vengeance has its own rewards. To destroy the Spanish, begin as before:

- Seal the Tlaxcalans off to the northwest, and take control of the central Gold deposit.
- Get onto the river early, and destroy the Spanish Galleons.
- Build for defense in the early going, and then speed toward a Castle and advancement to the Imperial Age.

After you mass resources and troops, including several Trebuchets, build a gate in the northwestern Stone Wall. Your first objective will be to seize the Stone and Gold deposits there *and hold them*. Although the Tlaxcalans aren't too tough if you have enough ranged weapons to whittle them down, expect the Spanish to show up to support them with heavier arms.

When you've established your beachhead on Tlaxcalan soil (as shown in Figure 6-11), build several Guard Towers and

Figure 6-11 *Mining the Tlaxcalans' Gold gives you the firepower you need to defeat the Spanish.*

stock them with ranged units for added defense. To your west you'll see an enemy Guard Tower and Gold Mine, both of which you should destroy. Claiming the Gold for your own devices should be your next move.

When you can move out and take possession of the large Gold deposit, send your Trebuchets along and have them start shelling the Tlaxcalan buildings on the western shore. Do all the damage you can, and try to bring out as many defenders as possible to make the city defenseless when you move in.

As you push across to the western shore and then northwest, take out the remaining buildings until the Tlaxcalans give up. Leave any walls that will help shelter you from Spanish raids intact; then fall back to your beachhead to regroup. Send more Villagers to mine the Gold—first by your Guard Towers and then later in the shallows.

Leave enough defensive forces around your working mine to deal with a Spanish attack, including a few Jaguar Warriors to chase down any Bombard Cannons, and some Pikemen to deal with heavy Spanish Cavalry. Leave a Monk, too, to heal up the defenders and to convert any units that might be helpful to the cause.

Send the rest of your offensive units back to your village for mending and healing. Add more Trebuchets and Eagle Warriors and Jaguar Warriors while you're there and a good number of Pikemen; send them all northeast through the pass to the Spanish Gate. Shell the towers, blow the gate, and slip into the Spanish rear area.

The main Spanish city sits across the river to the northwest, past the most distant corral. Before you rush ahead, have your Fire Ships scout the riverfront, and then send your troops there, but stop them just before they cross. Deploy your Trebuchets, take out the Castle to the west and the tower to the east, and use infantry to meet any counterattacks.

As you lose units, start building a second force around a group of Rams and Trebuchets. When they're ready for battle, send them north along the road from your Village while moving your Fire Ships to meet them at the shallows near the main gate to the Spanish city. Set up a second front there, and shell any enemy towers and buildings within range.

As you press on with each attack, keep a sharp eye out for Missionaries (Monks). Also, be careful any time you get close to a body of water. Spanish Galleons to the north are looking to reveal themselves at the worst possible moment.

As you close on and move through the main gate, sweeping northwest from the east, you'll come across another Castle (or two) and the main Spanish village. Lay siege, keeping defensive units between your

> **Tip:** *Hitting a Galleon with a Trebuchet can be almost impossible, unless the Galleon is paying attention to something else. Give yourself a better shot with your Trebuchets by using a fast Eagle Warrior on the shore to distract the enemy Galleon's attention.*

Figure 6-12   *Destroying the Spanish Town Center is the beginning of the end for the Conquistadors.*

Trebuchets and any Spanish attackers. When you fire on the Town Center, you have pushed into the heart of the city. (See Figure 6-12.)

Keep chasing down Villagers and Missionaries as you advance, but hang back when you near the sea. When you can distract any Galleons in wait for you, sneak a Villager up to the cove where Cortez sank his ships and build a Dock. Launch a few Fire Ships to hunt down the Galleons, and then turn your attention to any remaining Spanish forces. When you track down the last of the Spanish, you'll emerge the victor.

Mission Four: La Noche Triste

Objectives:

- Destroy the Spanish Wonder to end its influence in Tenochtitlan.

Hints:

- You'll need to sneak around Spanish and Tlaxcalan soldiers until you're ready to fight. Avoid conflict if you can.
- Use your Eagle Warriors to scout the path ahead. Use Pikemen to fight any Spanish Conquistadors you encounter.
- It's acceptable to damage the Tenochtitlan buildings even though they once belonged to your people. You can rebuild them after you drive out the Spanish.

Scout Reports:

- Because a single Aztec Jaguar Warrior leads the resistance, he must gather forces along the shores of Lake Texcoco before venturing into Tenochtitlan in the center.
- The Tlaxcala (red) have gathered in force along the north shore of the lake and along the causeways. They have many Eagle Warriors and a few Monks.
- The Spanish (blue) occupy Tenochtitlan. Their Conquistadors, Missionaries, and Mangonels could be trouble for the Aztec infantry.

First Walkthrough: Around the Lake

To destroy the Spanish Wonder and overthrow the Spanish seizure of Tenochtitlan, you need to rally support among the Aztec people. To begin, run southeast—avoiding Jaguars as usual—until you come across a small band of Aztec warriors who enlist in your cause. They also tell you of some prisoners in the north who might join your cause when they are freed.

Head your party north, past the pond where you began; then slow your march. Have several Eagle Warriors, whose line of sight is the best you have, probe slowly ahead, looking for enemy units. Soon you should discover three Tlaxcalan Eagle Warriors near the beach and a larger party of Jaguar Warriors guarding the end of a bridge. Take out the three Eagle Warriors to reveal two Transports just off the beach to the north. Seize the Transports, load your party, and then sail northwest, staying clear of the bridge. Go even slower now, given your shorter line of sight, until you reach the beach. Let an Eagle Warrior off as soon as possible to scout out your new position.

Ahead to the northwest, you'll see two Conquistadors, who might notice you as well. Don't do anything rash, withdraw, and scout a bit to the north. There, at the other end of the bridge, you'll find a well-armed Tlaxcalan party. Offload the whole of your army in secret, and then attack the Conquistadors, killing them as quickly as possible.

Moving on to the northwest and taking possession of an Outpost will increase your line of sight. Although the Jaguar pen nearby is interesting, you should keep your eyes on the Tlaxcalan Priest, in case he spots you before you can attack. Send some fast Eagle Warriors against the Priest to kill him before he can convert any of your units, and press on past the northern pen to take possession of an Onager and Outpost.

> **Tip:** *It pays to keep your heavily injured units out of further trouble until you can heal them. You might even want to create a separate formation of injured units so that you can call them away from battle with one command.*

Head northeast now, and use ranged weapons to soften up the party of Tlaxcalan Jaguar Warriors that stand in your way before you engage them in hand-to-hand combat. Mass your ranged weapons on individual targets, and take out the others with infantry groups. When you're done, make a quick charge northeast until you hook up with a small band of Eagle Warriors eager for your cause.

As you continue northeast, take out three Tlaxcalan Eagle Warriors guarding a Barracks, and then destroy the barracks while you have a lone Eagle Warrior scout ahead. Avoid the Guard Tower off the beach, and when you spot the prisoners, bring the rest of your troops up to break out the prisoners.

Mass all of your units away from the Tlaxcalan Castle to the northeast of the bridge, and then send one Eagle Warrior at full speed toward the dock that was revealed near Tenochtitlan. Avoid fire from an Aztec War Galley to the north; when you get to the Dock, have your Eagle Warrior jump aboard one of the waiting Transports. If the War Galley appears, use the two Fast Fire Ships you commandeered to destroy it, and then send all your ships up to the northwest end of the bridge.

Load all of your troops, and sail around to the southeast. Be sure to give Tenochtitlan a wide berth. Aim for the small green torch revealed to you in the southeast. Unload your troops there, and send an Eagle Warrior to scout the torch. When you reveal a city surrounding a Shrine, you encounter two Priests who will join you. (See Figure 6-13.) Immediately begin researching Block Printing at the Shrine, and build two more Priests.

Send your Fire Ships to scout around Tenochtitlan, and have them take out any ships they come across, particularly Spanish Cannon Galleons. (If you lose the Fire Ships, don't worry; you won't need them any longer.)

Scout to the southwest until you find the twin bridges leading to Tenochtitlan, and have an Eagle Warrior run up the bridge until he's within view of the city.

Figure 6-13 *You won't find Villagers in this city, but Priests are the next best thing.*

Have him scout around carefully to get the lay of the land; while doing so, send your two original Priests up to join him. When they arrive, move them off to the left toward the gate, leading with the Eagle Warrior so as to give the Monks the greatest line of sight. When an enemy Villager seems a likely candidate, have the Priests convert the unit.

If you get a Villager, have him come around toward you to the south, and put him to work building a Siege Workshop near the two Spanish Docks. While he's building the Siege Workshop, bring all your forces up to your position, keeping an eye out for ships sailing close to the bridges from the north.

> **Tip:** *Conversion is not a sure thing, and you should be careful not to do it when the Villager is too far away from you. Plenty of Spanish units are waiting to chop a converted Villager to pieces, meaning you'll have wasted your time and Faith.*

After you build the Siege Workshop, upgrade to Capped Rams, and then move your army toward the opening in the fence to the north. Lure enemy defenders toward you, and destroy them as quickly as possible while staying away from the withering Castle fire. Convert any Conquistadors that you can and turn them to your own ends; make sure you clean out the city. When you're sure the coast is clear, build two Capped Rams and send them against the Wonder. (See Figure 6-14.)

> **Tip:** *If you're running short of time, send some infantry up to the Rams and garrison them inside. Not only will the Rams travel faster, but you'll have defenders ready in case you missed a foe somewhere.*

Direct the Rams to attack the Wonder on the side farthest from the two Castles, and then hammer away until the Wonder falls and your people are free!

Figure 6-14   *Despite their slow pace, and fire from the enemy castle, these Rams are up to the task.*

AGE *of* EMPIRES II

Second Walkthrough: The Runner

Speed is of the essence! While you're making plans, the enemy Wonder is growing more difficult to destroy. Send your Jaguar Warrior northwest, hook him up with an Eagle Warrior, and head them both northwest. When you encounter three enemy Eagle Warriors, sprint past them and onto the waiting Transport ships, and then set sail to the northwest. Don't stop until you hit the beach.

Note: *If you're gong to get to the Wonder early, don't waste any time thinking while the clock is ticking. If you need to plan a move, hit the F3 key to pause the game.*

At the beach, unload the Eagle Warrior only, and have him move north until the Conquistador guards spot him. Run the Eagle Warrior north to decoy the Conquistadors, and send an empty Transport ship north along the beach at the same time. When the Conquistadors give chase and the Tlaxcalan units at the bridge are closing in, load the Eagle Warrior back on the Transport and sail him southeast before looping back to join the Jungle Warrior still waiting aboard the second ship. Offload your units, and sneak them northwest, behind the Conquistadors' backs. (See Figure 6-15.)

Head northeast until you discover the pen of Jaguars. Blow open the wall in the east, and move forward until you expose the waiting Tlaxcalan Priest. Let the Jaguars have a quick bite while you back off to stay out of the Priest's range; now wait until the Jaguars wander off.

Head around the pen to the north, and take possession of an

Figure 6-15   *After you distract the Conquistadors, you should be able to slip by unnoticed.*

Onager. Move the Onager east, and turn it loose on the group of enemy Jaguar Warriors as a distraction while you slip your two infantry by along the north-western slope. Race ahead until you join up with a group of loyal Eagle Warriors, and head everybody out into the shallows around the barracks. Aim for the prisoners and their release!

Break the prisoners out, and then take out the group of Tlaxcalan Arbalests that attack from the bridge to the southeast. Defeat them quickly, and send one Eagle Warrior down the bridge toward the Dock that has been revealed at Tenochtitlan. When the ships near the Dock are revealed, have the Eagle Warrior jump on a Transport and send the whole fleet to the northeast, avoiding the city. Sailing east and then south-east toward the solitary torch, turn your First Ships back to take care of any enemy vessels that give chase. You'll want the seas quiet when you return.

> **Tip:** *Stay away from the city in your ships! If two Castles firing a hail of arrows isn't bad enough, War Galleys and Cannon Ships are waiting to scuttle your plans.*

Let your Eagle Warrior off, and have him discover the small village and Shrine as quickly as possible. Immediately send the Eagle Warrior and two Priests north-west along the bridge to Tenochtitlan, and take note of the Lumber Camp they find there. Move two Transport Ships close to the southern end of the bridge in anticipation of taking on cargo.

When you reach the edge of the city, have the two Priests convert a Villager coming out to drop wood off at the Lumber Camp. As soon as you do so, send the Villager back down the bridge to your southeast, and have the Priests and your Eagle Warrior take on any Conquistadors that try to give chase. Your Villager must get away!

Now send all of your troops and freed Prisoners down the bridge toward the city. Take out the Conquistadors near the Dock, and do your best to get two siege engines to come after you—at least one of which is just inside a wall near the Wonder. You'll take some casualties, but it's important to get rid of those siege engines.

At the southern end of the bridge, have the Villager build a Siege Workshop and then four Rams. Load two Rams on one Transport each, and sail the ships back around to the north, giving the city a wide berth once again. While on the lake, upgrade the Rams to Capped Rams at the Siege Workshop.

AGE *of* EMPIRES II

Figure 6-16   *If you've been fast, you might knock down Cortez's Wonder with only these two Rams.*

When your Transports are north of the city, land them one at a time just northwest of the northern-most Castle. (See Figure 6-16.) Get the first two Rams off fast before the Castles sink your ship, and send them after the Wonder immediately. While the first Rams are on their way and taking fire, slip the second ship in and unload.

With the enemy siege engines destroyed by your troops, you shouldn't face any defenses other than the arrows from the Castles. Your Rams should be able to take everything the Castles dish out, and more, while on the way to destroying the Wonder.

Mission Five: The Boiling Lake

Objectives:

- Defeat the Tlaxcalans and Spanish.

Hints:

- This far from Tenochtitlan, you are cut off from your resources and will have to search for additional Gold and Stone.
- Spanish Cannon Galleons are deadly. Do not lose your navy on Lake Texcoco or risk shore bombardment.
- Tlaxcalan Jaguar Warriors are adept at defeating Aztec infantry. It's a pity the Aztecs have been unable to domesticate horses.

Scout Reports:

- The Aztecs (green) begin on an island in Lake Texcoco in pursuit of flee-ing Spanish (blue) and Tlaxcalans (red).
- The two enemies have a combined fortress to the north of the lake that requires a considerable army to penetrate.
- You can garner additional resources east and west of the lake, but if you do not focus enough on a navy, the Spanish will be able to level your en-tire town with their ships.

First Walkthrough: The Fruits of the Jungle

A lot is going on here, so plan on taking your time and making deliberate choices and troop movements early. The more you falter in the beginning, the harder it's going to be to pull even with your enemies, let alone achieve victory. Note the following:

- The proximity of your forces to the fleeing Spanish means you're going to get action from the get-go. Change all your forces from an Aggressive to Defensive stance, and group them so that they are under positive control.
- You start with Elite Jaguar Warriors, Elite Eagle Warriors, and Arbalests, but you won't be able to actually build those same units until you upgrade. Don't throw this very tough force away on a cheap payback.
- Your main fortress in the east is well protected and houses some important structures, but it has zero access to resources. Treat it as a factory, and de-fend it for that reason, but don't try to improve it.
- Your Town Center and many of your houses are on an incredibly vulner-able island, with every building at risk from offshore bombardment. You need to make heavy use of the three Docks there, so plan on keeping them around a while.
- You have a lot of buildings built for you *but no Blacksmith*! Make sure you don't forget to build one because you need him to attain some important infantry upgrades.
- The "Lake" you face is mostly shallows, which means ships *and* land units can attack with relative ease. Although you can't get away from land forces, you can get away from ships in the west, which is a good reason to go there.

When play begins, have at the Spaniards, but do so under control. Chew them up, along with the Tlaxcalan force waiting to rescue them, but try to save enough of your troops to use as a defensive force back at your fortress.

On your way back home, have an Eagle Warrior scout out the eastern terrain. When you come across two carts of Spanish Powder, send them to the Plaza in front of your Castle (marked by six torches). You'll net two Bombard Cannons for your trouble, which you should make the centerpiece of your defensives force.

Meanwhile, at your Town Center, send all your existing Villagers to the far west and build another five to work on the surrounding Farms that have already been seeded. Keep them farming except when they need to fix a leaky ship. When your Villagers arrive in the far west, have them break the Horses out of the Palisade they'll find there; then get to work building a Town Center nearby, back from the main jungle paths. Send the Horses to the plaza.

At your new Town Center in the west, build a Lumber Camp and then a Gold Mine just to the east. Build more Villagers, too, and start putting in more Farms. This new Town Center will be the source of all of your power for a good long time, so send some defenders there as soon as you can or build them on site.

Although you might want to put up walls and other fortifications, for the time being stay lean and quiet. Enemy forces might knock down a tower or two, but if you're tucked away, they probably won't find you—or your Gold Mine. Have a fast-reaction force handy just in case, but keep as low a profile as possible. (See Figure 6-17.)

At the Docks, upgrade to Fast Fire Ships and start launching them in a one-to-one ratio with War Galleys. Build a lot of them, but don't send them anywhere; you'll be getting plenty of visitors at your little island, and you need to keep it functioning while you're building your resource juggernaut in the west. When you're not under attack, add more houses on the island as well until you can field your maximum force of 150 units.

When you receive your Elite Tarkans, route them back to the west and have them break down the gate penning in the second group of horses near your new Town Center. Route those Horses to the Plaza, and join them with your first group of Tarkans.

As you bring in Gold, build a Blacksmith in the west, if you don't have one, so that you can upgrade to Bracer, Plate Mail, and Blast Furnace. Upgrade to Arbalests at

an Archery Range, and then build enough ranged units to do some damage, especially at your new Town Center. Build a Shrine in the west, and station two Priests there and in the east; then research Block Printing and Illumination. At your Castle, research Garland Wars and Conscription.

Figure 6-17   *Even without protective walls, you should be able to mine all of this Gold in peace.*

When you have the resources freed up, build an expeditionary force of two Trebuchets and enough infantry to keep the enemy at bay. Push north from your fortress into enemy territory, staying off the beach. Push northwest to look for two more groups of Horses penned inside Fortified Walls, and free them as soon as you can. Send them all back to the plaza, and reap more Elite Tarkans for your cause.

While you're freeing the horses, probe the enemy's defenses a bit, but don't get too close to the shore or the main Tlaxcalan encampment. Also note any Gold deposits that you might be able to use to your own ends later. When the horses are free and you're pretty confident that you know where the eastern entrance to the Tlaxcalan city is, return and heal up at the fortress while you gather more resources.

> **Tip:** *You're going to be irritated by the presence of the Spanish Bombard Tower in the west, and you're going to want to take it out. Don't. You're not going to be launching an attack from the west, so there's little point.*

> **Tip:** *If the goal is mining all the Gold as fast as possible, it makes sense that more Villagers mean you'll spend less time out there in the open waiting for Cannon Ships to wander by and find your range. Put a bunch of Villagers to the task!*

When your first Gold deposits run out, send your miners and some guard troops to the Gold-rich island. While you clear away the Jaguars and get to mining, send a good-sized fleet to protect the island from Spanish ships. Although you can almost certainly keep the enemy from overrunning your position, you have to be vigilant.

Tip: *Watch out for Spanish on the beach! The island with four Bombard Towers on it effectively screens your navy from joining the attack on the main Tlaxcalan buildings. That means you have to walk a tightrope between the Spanish-held shore and the mountains, trying to attract as little attention as possible from either direction.*

Close in your western town now, if you haven't, by fortifying it with walls and a good number of ranged defenders. Make sure you have a gate handy so that you can get out in the face of long-range Spanish weapons, and keep an eye on your Lumberjacks so that they don't inadvertently open up access to your city by cutting down the wrong trees.

From here on out you need to keep attacking the enemy out of your fortress, using Trebuchets to break through fortifications and raze Towers. As you wade into the complex of defenses that the Tlaxcalans and Spanish have set up, you'll see that the Tlaxcalans are along the lake, with the Spanish in a fortified mountain retreat to the north.

Your number one priority should be getting the Tlaxcalans to throw in the towel—you don't want to have to keep them off your flank while you're trying to dig the Spanish out. When you're pressing in on the Tlaxcalan Town Center and Castle from the east, secure a position and then shell the structures from a distance with your Trebuchets. Having plenty of upgraded Elite Jaguar Warriors around should keep your heavy artillery relatively safe; in time, the Tlaxcalan resistance will run out.

When the Tlaxcalans fall, turn your attention to the two gates giving access to the Spanish stronghold. Shell the single gate to the east until it falls, and take on the double gates and towers in the west—but only as a distraction. The nearby Spanish Castle will field some Trebuchets in response, which is when you should rush the double gates with some upgraded Rams. (See Figure 6-18.)

Figure 6-18 *Send your Rams against the gate and then through it when the enemy comes to meet them!*

As enemy forces come out of the gates, you should be able to sneak your Rams in against the Castle, by which time they'll be too close for Trebuchets to fire. Bring your own Trebuchets up from the blown eastern gate, and lay siege to the city. If you've prepared sufficient stockpiles, Montezuma's death will soon be avenged.

Second Walkthrough: The Hammer of the Gods

Follow the instructions in the first walkthrough, until you have freed all the Spanish Horses and have just begun mining the small, Gold-rich island. After you convert all of the Horses to Elite Tarkans and you have enough houses to allow you to build to your 150-unit maximum, send almost all of your forces, including all of your Tarkans, Trebuchets, Jaguar Warriors, and Eagle Warriors, to your new village in the west. (Route them south to keep them out of enemy territory.)

In the west, start building your new village into a serious war machine. Add a new Archery Range, Barracks, and Siege Workshop so that you can build new forces on the spot, and then upgrade to Siege Rams and Elite Eagle Warriors. Back at your fortress, upgrade Jaguar Warriors to Elite status and research Garland Wars to give them punch.

Build fifteen Elite Jaguar Warriors, and send them west via your old Town Center. Build fifteen Elite Eagle Warriors at your new Barracks in the west, along with five Siege Rams at your new Siege Workshop. When the Jaguar Warriors arrive, load them into the Siege Rams in equal measure with Eagle Warriors until all five Rams are full.

With a complement of ranged weapons and three or four Priests at the ready, move your Trebuchets forward and blast the Spanish Bombard Tower to your northeast. As soon as it falls, run an Eagle Warrior past to scout around for enemy units that stand in your way. The objective is a quiet route through the jungle that leads to the edge of the Tlaxcalan city. Have some Villagers come out and begin mining the Stone deposits just to the east, if they aren't doing so already.

Note: *You won't have to knock down any walls to get into the city from this direction, but you also won't run across any Gold deposits to mine. Keep an eye on your Gold reserves, and spend wisely. What you take off the island should do.*

Push northeast until you come across the five Spanish powder wagons. Send them west, southwest, and then north to your plaza. There convert them into Bombard Cannons. Keep advancing your main force, and try to get the Siege Rams in against the Tlaxcalan Castle as cleanly as you can. When it falls, attack other nearby structures to clear out that end of the town. (See Figure 6-19.)

When a Ram is destroyed, make use of its infantry payload to keep enemy units from attacking the other Rams. When the Spanish and Tlaxcalans counterattack, pull your forces back and use ranged fire to greet the pursuers while you augment your

Figure 6-19 *With the Castle fallen, your Rams should be able to take out the Tlaxcalan Town Center.*

Figure 6-20 *Your Rams will decimate the Spanish city after they breach its defensive fortifications.*

depleted forces with new units from the west. With good attack orders, your Rams should chew up most of the western end of the Tlaxcalan territory.

Build a Castle near the farther Stone deposits toward the northeast, and use it to anchor your next assault force. Stock it with a few ranged units to add defensive cover, and crank out a few new Trebuchets if you need them. Rebuild your Jaguar Warrior and Eagle Warrior forces, and load them in Siege Rams as before.

Run an Eagle Warrior to the northeast to look for the double-gated entrance to the Spanish stronghold. When you know where it is, blow it open with your Trebuchets and send your Rams in against the Castle nearby. Destroy the Castle as quickly as you can; then press into the stronghold, and take on the Spanish Town Center. (See Figure 6-20.) Follow your Rams with ranged forces and infantry (especially Pikemen) as well as Priests.

Gut the Spanish city while overrunning it. Press the attack until Cortez surrenders; then swing eastward and crash out the gate against whatever Tlaxcalan forces and structures remain. In short order, the Tlaxcalans will follow Cortez into oblivion.

Mission Six: Broken Spears

Objectives:

- Defeat the Tlaxcala, the Spanish Army, and the Spanish Navy.

Hints:

- Tenochtitlan is a vast city. However, there are multiple buildings of each type, so it should be easy to train units or research upgrades.
- Defend the bridges into the great city from Spanish and Tlaxcalan land attacks, but also train ships to defend against Spanish warships and Transports. Spanish Cannon Galleons can be deadly.

Scout Reports:

- The Aztecs (green) are back in control of the great city of Tenochtitlan, but enemies are approaching from all sides.
- The Tlaxcalans (red) attack from the western causeway. Their poorly fortified city might fall to an early attack.
- The Spanish Navy is south of Tenochtitlan. The Spanish have many Cannon Galleons patrolling the Lake, and their shore is defended by Bombard Towers. It still might be possible to locate an undefended landing spot.
- The Spanish Army is just to the north of Tenochtitlan. The Spanish have constructed gates and Castles to defend their forces. Expect to encounter Knights, Conquistadors, Missionaries, and Bombard Cannons. The Spanish use Transports if they cannot attack from the land.

First Walkthrough: Dancing Across the Water

Before you do anything, plug the leak that is the open bridge to your southwest. Not only will Tlaxcalan Eagle Warriors be sprinting into your city in mere seconds, but Cortez's army will be using the bridge as well, circumventing your Stone Wall and gate in the northwest. Have your villagers close off the bridge with a solid Stone Wall, and, as always, make sure it's actually closed off.

Put your other Villagers to work mining Gold and Stone and, especially, chopping Wood—even though you start out with a goodly amount. Build a few Fishing Boats to take advantage of the Fishing Traps to the east, too, but don't go overboard. Your maximum number of units is 75, which means you won't be able to field a huge army and keep resources pouring in.

Upgrade to Shipwright immediately at your northernmost Dock, and at the two Docks in the east start launching a fifty-fifty mix of War Galleys and Fire Ships. Upgrade to Fast Fire ships as soon as you have ten ships in the water, and send your first fleet to watch over the fishing boats to the east. You're going to be contesting those waters for some time to come, so be prepared to build and fix a lot of ships.

When Cortez's navy appears, don't be timid about sinking his boats. Stay away from his shoreline, where Bombard Towers are waiting to hurt you, but beyond that sink every Spanish ship you can get your guns on. When you have twenty or so boats forming a blockade, you should be able to keep your fleet healthy by fixing the few ships that take heavy damage. Don't back down, and don't stop building new ships!

When there's a lull, or when you're running out of Gold in your city, send a ship north to scout out the island full of Gold. While you're up there, scout out the seas to the northwest, where you discover three Turtle Ships that you can put to very good use. Send the Turtle Ships back to your Docks, but keep them out of harm's way for now.

When you're out of Gold, transport your miners up to the Gold island. As long as you keep the Spanish Navy engaged, it won't be attacking your island and you can probably strip it without being discovered.

At the next lull, send your Turtle ships and War Galleys in to attack one of the two Spanish Docks along the Spanish coast to the east. (See Figure 6-21.) Watch out for Bombard Towers and for ships spawning at the Docks, but do your best to destroy at least one of the Docks before you withdraw for repairs.

Figure 6-21   *Your Turtle Ships can shell the Spanish Docks from out of Bombard Tower range.*

When you've knocked both of the Spanish Docks out of commission, the Spanish lands to the east will be yours for the taking, although you'll have to put up a fight. Get to them quickly, and you might be able to claim a fair amount of Gold deposits, too.

> **Note:** *If you hear a Missionary (Spanish Monk) conjuring, pull your Turtle Ships back immediately and then determine what's going on. Although Turtle Ships can take a lot of damage, one Missionary can sink a Turtle Ship in a flash because you begin with Heresy already researched.*

At each end of the Spanish Navy's coastline, there's a bit of beach where you can land a transport and not be under fire from Bombard Towers. Load two Trebuchets each in a transport, flank each transport with some War Galleys and a few Fast Fire Ships, and send one Armada to each end of the Spanish shore. Unload the Trebuchets at each end, and move them along the shoreline just enough so that they can target their first Bombard Towers. Make sure the Trebuchets stay on the beach to get cover fire from the escort ship, and set the ships to Defensive Stance so that they don't change enemy units into the range of a tower.

You should take out the first two Bombard Towers without too much trouble. In the south, if you see a Gold Mine, take it out, too, and then move up the beach at each end, drawing a bead on the next Bombard Towers. Press your attack, and if your Trebuchets get chewed up, consider transporting them back to your city for repair, if only to save the Gold it would take to replace them. If you do dock at home to make repairs, consider including some Pikemen on the return trip to attack the Conquistadors and Missionaries that are gunning for your artillery.

Although you'll probably be under no other direct threats, don't dawdle. Wipe out the navy town as quickly as possible to conserve your stockpiles and the enemy's unexploited resources. When the Spanish Navy does go down, prepare for an immediate escalation of activity from the Spanish Army, which will have gotten the word.

When the Spanish Army comes on in force (as shown in Figure 6-22), your ships are going to do you little good. If you have plenty of food (and you should), scuttle a good number of your fishing boats to create more Eagle Warriors, Jaguar Warriors, and Pikemen. Consider researching Conscription at the Castle to speed up deployment.

> **Tip:** *Don't forget to upgrade your infantry at the Blacksmith and to research Garland Wars at your Castle. The Spanish Army is mostly cavalry and very tough.*

Try to keep the Spanish Army behind your walls by using your Trebuchets and some Onagers to destroy them before they ever get a chance to hack their way inside. If they do get in your city, call up a ton of upgraded Pikemen and back them with Jaguar Warriors and Eagle Warriors. In any case, prepare to meet a lot of horses coming your way.

Figure 6-22 *If the fast Spanish cavalry breaks out, you'll have a hard time hunting them down.*

When the Spanish Army slows its advance, send your Trebuchets and any Turtle Ships you have left to knock down their main gate. You'll unleash a violent counterattack, but, again, plenty of Pikemen and Jaguar Warriors should be able to hold their own. If all seems lost, fall back, regroup, and try again.

When you crack the Spanish Army's defenses, load up some Capped Rams with Pikemen and send them in under guard to attack the Town Center. Veer away from the Castle to keep your guard units from being pincushioned with arrows, and take down the Town Center and as many other buildings in the northern part of the city as possible. Although resistance will be strong at first, you should be able to wear the army down, take out its Castle with Trebuchets, and get an unconditional surrender. Which means it's time to blow a hole in your wall to the south, and take on the Tlaxcalans.

> **Note:** *Don't waste time shelling your wall or trying to hack it down. Just select the section of wall you want to remove, and hit the Delete key to make a small exit.*

Although the Tlaxcalans are pretty straightforward, they're also pretty tough. You'll face a few upgraded Scorpions, but the toughest fight will be going up against fully upgraded Eagle Warriors and Jaguar Warriors like your own. To gain a bit of an advantage, field plenty of ranged units in a squad so that they can soften the enemy up before the infantry meets them in hand-to-hand combat. As much as possible, try to use your own Jaguar Warriors on the enemy's Eagle Warriors; follow up with Trebuchets to take out important buildings.

After you take out the two Barracks, the Siege Workshop, and the first Castle, you should be able to clean up fairly quickly because the Tlaxcalans will starve for defensive units. Bring in some Rams and turn them loose, covering them with ranged fire, and soon Tenochtitlan will be safe from enemy conquest.

Second Walkthrough: In Defense of a City

Surrounded on three sides by marauders, your glorious city of Tenochtitlan is naked to conquest. To ensure its survival, you must enclose the city in a wall of stone, a wall your enemies will have to conquer before they can hope to conquer you.

Begin by sending all but two of your Villagers to build Fortified Walls on the beaches around your city. Distribute the remaining two Villagers at the Stone Mine in the north to mine Stone; you'll need a ready supply. Build your first wall to close the causeway to the southwest—as always, make sure no one can still slip through somewhere.

> **Note:** *Build walls not only along the lake, but also up waterways until you reach a bridge. Any opening, no matter how small, invites an enemy landing.*

While you're putting your first Villagers to work on defenses, build another group at each Town Center and get them started on Gold, Wood, and Food. You're going to be daring your enemies to attack and trying to get them to burn through their resources when they do so. Early on, pay particular attention to Gold because the city has a limited supply. Don't spend any more than you have to on defending yourself.

Take advantage of some Fishing Traps to your east. The Spanish Navy will contest your possession of them, and although you should meet its challenge, go no further. From now until your other enemies fall before you, you should simply keep the Spanish Navy at arm's reach without going on the offensive.

You'll suffer a few early attacks and landings, but you should be able to cut the enemy down and enclose your city. Additionally, the Spanish Army will probe your northern gate, which you should simply seal closed with a second Fortified Wall if it looks like they're going to try to break through. In the east, the Spanish Navy will attack your Watch Towers and Docks, but good defensive tactics should limit any real damage.

To augment your initial forces, add a dozen Pikemen in case the Spanish Army does find a way to enter. Research Garland Wars at the Castle and Plate Mail Armor and Blast Furnace at the Blacksmith.

When your city is closed in and you're finally out of Gold at your Town Center, build a transport and load some Villagers aboard. (See Figure 6-23.) Sail the Transport north to the island loaded with Gold, and have the Villagers get to work. Next send the Transport northwest to discover the three Turtle Ships, and then station the Turtle Ships east of the island to fight off any attacking Spanish vessels.

When you're bringing in sufficient Gold, build a force of Pikemen and ferry them up to the shallows northeast of the Spanish Army's territory. Paladins and other Cavalry will be there, so loose your Pikemen upon them and wipe them out.

While that's going on, build two Trebuchets and some more Pikemen. Upgrade to Elite Jaguar Warriors and build a half dozen of them, and upgrade to Siege Rams and build four. When your Pikemen have taken the shallows, have them wait while you send the two Trebuchets and some of the reinforcements to join them.

Figure 6-23 *Pull your Transport up to a bridge, and load your units through the bow one at a time.*

Figure 6-24 *Your Pikemen will keep enemy cavalry at bay until the Trebuchets have done their work.*

Eliminate the Spanish Army's ability to replenish cavalry by using the Trebuchets to destroy the two Stables inside the city walls. (See Figure 6-24.) Ferry the Rams over while using the Trebuchets to blow the northeast city gate in anticipation of their arrival.

From here on out you need only make a slow, methodical march of destruction to the southwest, through the Spanish Army's town. When the army surrenders, swing southeast without breaking stride toward the Tlaxcalan city in the south. Chew up the Tlaxcalan forces and buildings up as you go. If you need ranged support, send Arbalests down from Tenochtitlan. When you approach the first of the Tlaxcalan Castles, send your Rams in again, and have Jaguar Warriors ready to deal with counterattacking infantry from the south.

By this time the Spanish Navy should be falling silent as they run out of Gold, so take your time finishing off the Tlaxcalans. When the Tlaxcalans surrender, move against the Spanish Navy's fortifications and give no quarter.

Chapter Seven

···>

THE ATTILA THE HUN CAMPAIGN

In a two-year period, Attila the Hun rose from virtual anonymity to being a feared world conqueror. Leaving horrific hoof prints in the withering wake of his mounted march across central Europe, Attila banded together warring factions and brought them to the brink of power with his uncompromising and unyielding will. Despite the brevity of his time as a dominant leader, Attila the Hun ensured his place in history because of the prize he sought, the ferocity with which he pursued it, and his eventual success.

In the Attila the Hun campaign, you retrace Attila's greatest and most brutal battles, beginning with a portent of his thirst for power and rule and ending with his greatest victory against the Roman Empire. Where before Goths, Scythians, and Romans existed, by the time you emerge victorious only the Huns, and those who saw fit to join them, will have survived.

Mission One: The Scourge of God

Objectives:

- Attila must survive.
- Attila must make sure Bleda is killed and then must return to the Huns' camp.
- *Then* you must defeat two of your remaining three enemies (the Scythians, Romans, and Persians).

Hints:

- You can defeat Bleda in several ways: you can change your stance with him to Enemy and attack him, you can see that he dies in an accident, or you can refuse his challenge altogether and flee the Huns' camp.
- Look for allies in unlikely places. The Scythians are not on good terms with the Romans, so it might be possible to convince the two to fight against each other.
- The Huns can reach the Castle Age only.

AGE
of
EMPIRES II

Scout Reports:

- Attila the Hun (yellow) initially commands no troops because all of the Huns are loyal to the Hunnic king, Bleda, who is Attila's brother. Attila must somehow depose Bleda to inherit troops and villagers.
- Three other enemies are scattered across the landscape. The Western Roman Empire (blue) has a fort to the south where it holds some Huns captive. The Romans rely on their infantry for combat.
- The Scythians (green) have a scattered encampment to the west. Because the Scythians are a nomadic people, unmined reserves of Stone remain in their area.
- The most dangerous enemy is the Persian city across the bay to the east. The Persians (pink) hoard lots of Gold, but their army consists of Mangonels and War Elephants, as well as a considerable navy.

First Walkthrough: Forging an Alliance

Your brother, Bleda, grumbling about your apparent desire to lead the Huns, offers a challenge to see which of you can kill the nearby Iron Boar. With rule over the Huns at stake, Bleda knows you cannot refuse, particularly in front of your Tarkans. Following Bleda into the woods, you prepare for the challenge, regardless of the risk.

Tip: *Although you can maneuver so that Bleda takes most of the damage and ends up killing the boar himself, this only causes dissension when you arrive back at camp. Take a few lumps, and kill the boar yourself to keep your Tarkans from fighting amongst themselves. You start with more and healthier units that way.*

Note: *You must change your diplomatic stance to get your Tarkans to attack Bleda and his assassins!*

After you kill the boar and reveal Bleda's treacherous plans, return to the camp and the waiting Tarkans. The Tarkans recognize Bleda's duplicity and willingly join you against his assassins. Use the Tarkans to attack and kill your treacherous sibling and his henchmen, after which you become leader of the Huns!

When the camp is yours, put the three Villagers you inherited to work where they stand, to cut Wood, gather Food, and mine Stone. Build a fourth Villager to mine the nearby Gold, and advance your civilization to the Feudal Age.

When you return to camp, a Villager tells you of some hostages held by the Romans, whose freedom Bleda had been negotiating. This is a good time to note that

you have a single Cavalry Scout loitering afield and itching to look around. Change the Scout's attack stance to Stand Ground, and direct him south to get the lay of the land.

When your Scout catches sight of Roman troops, they let you know that Bleda's deal is off. In response, send all your troops south across the river, along the road to the Roman city, and don't be distracted by Roman units or other forces along the way. While traveling south, you might spot some Horses and notice that there are two different kinds of them. You can control a Horse unit after you spot it, and you should send any Horses you come across to your village for safekeeping. You cannot control the Wild Horse, and later it proves to be a real pain.

> **Note:** *Don't have the Scout enter the Roman city. If he spots the Villagers, they become fair game for enemy forces, which means you won't have anyone to rescue by the time you get your troops down there. Enter the Roman city only when you're ready to rescue the captives and fight your way out.*

When you arrive at the Roman city, enter through the front gate and head southwest until you spot the hostages. (See Figure 7-1.) Free the Villagers by using a few Tarkans, and send the rest of your forces to crush any opposition.

Soon a hostage Scythian Scout calls to you from a nearby Palisade. In exchange for freeing him from the Romans, the Scout promises a reward, so free him along with the Villagers. After he's free, the Scout proposes a truce and suggests that you send Attila northwest to the Scythian camp to talk about a permanent alliance. Send Attila immediately to the Scythian camp, and have him ignore any fire taken from the Scythian forces along the way. While Attila rides, herd the freed Villagers northwest, toward a small westerly

Figure 7-1   *Those Villagers and that Scythian Scout quickly change the balance of power.*

opening in a thick patch of forest. Once there, guide the Villagers inside and begin collecting the considerable resources you discover. (See Figure 7-2.)

Figure 7-2 *Without a Scythian alliance, those rich deposits are almost impossible to seize.*

When Attila arrives at the camp, the Scythian leader proposes an alliance contingent upon the delivery of ten Horses. Send all the Horses you have at your village, including the three in the Palisade north of your Town Center, to the flagged Scythian Palisade that's revealed to you. If you don't have ten, scout around and find others as soon as you can because they net you a large force of Heavy Cavalry Archers and the sworn alliance of the Scythians. When you forge the Scythian alliance, the Persians remain your only threat, even if the feeble Roman town has not yet admitted defeat.

> **Tip:** *Your Villager chopping wood at your base camp is very close to a pair of Horses, but don't loiter when you find them. The Persians are near, and they have a long reach from the sea.*

When you have sufficient resources, advance to the Castle Age and set your sights on building a Castle. You need it primarily to heal your troops quickly and safely but also to build more Tarkans. Concentrate now on defense and the improvement of your city.

If they haven't already, at some point those pesky Wild Horses spook your gift Horses out of the Palisade, which prompts the Scythians to ask you to round them up. Do so promptly—they won't go far—and send a Villager to close up the Palisade.

If you're still tangling with the Romans, send any injured units back to your home camp to defend against marauding Persians and have them stay in your

Castle until healed. Send a few Heavy Cavalry Archers to join the camp as defenders, but send the bulk of them to the Roman city with your Tarkans and lay waste to the town.

When the Romans surrender, heal and upgrade your units; then start picking off Persian units and outposts away from the main Persian fortress. Build a Siege Workshop and a few Mangonels, and use them to help take down that irritating Persian Guard Tower east of your Village and to destroy the Gold Mine there as well.

> **Note:** *You're going to want to become familiar with grouping your units so that you can control them with a single key. If you're not doing it already, group the Heavy Cavalry Archers together and have them attack any Roman units that appear. Group the Tarkans together, and have them demolish the important Roman buildings.*

Keep gathering resources, massing troops, and scouring your lands for Persian troops to pick off. When you have the might, aim for the Persian city itself, destroying any outlying structures or units along the way. Either the Persians see the writing on the wall and surrender, or you arrive with more than enough might to defeat them.

Second Walkthrough: Fighting Fire with Water

Of the three foes you face, the Scythians in the west and the Persians in the east are very real threats and you can all but ignore the Romans in the south. Other than sending a small force of infantry against you from time to time, the Romans keep to themselves, whereas the other two combatants do not. The Scythians are a potent force and quite close. The Persians are

> **Tip:** *If you build a Castle close to the nearby Persian Guard Tower, increase the range of Archers by upgrading at the Archery Range; the Castle's defensive fire will take down the tower.*

more removed, but they pack an even greater wallop, which they *do* deliver. To defeat them each in turn, you need to concentrate early on defense and on an economy that churns out considerable Food and Wood.

Upgrade to the Castle Age, and build a Castle in the gap to the south of your Town Center as soon as possible. Then, to funnel attacks into that avenue of approach, build a Stone Wall from the bridge to the patch of forest to your southwest, closing off access to your rear. (See Figure 7-3.)

For defense now and offense later, build Skirmishers and Spearmen and upgrade them to Elite Skirmishers and Pikemen as soon as possible. Although a bit slow, the Scythians make heavy use of Archers, which the Skirmishers enjoy

Figure 7-3   *Building a Stone Wall here funnels enemy attacks into the teeth of your defenses.*

Figure 7-4   *The arrows from those Guard Towers won't slow your Rams at all.*

skewering, and the Persians favor Cavalry, which your Pikemen can quickly gut. Another advantage to Skirmishers and Pikemen is that they don't require Gold, which is in short supply until you wipe out the Scythians and gain uncontested access to the riches in the clearing south of their village. Use any Gold you have sparingly for key upgrades and then later for Rams to take on the Scythian Castle—but only after the Scythian resistance has been worn down. (See Figure 7-4.)

After you defeat the Scythians, you gain access to the resources you need to build a force capable of taking on the Persian stronghold. Be ready to defend against the occasional War Elephant while you build your force of arms, and remember to build a good number of Pikemen.

Mission Two: The Great Ride

Objectives:

- Raid the Roman villages. When you have enough resources to build a forward base, you can field an army against the Romans.
- *Then* train an army and defeat the Romans by leveling their Town Center.

Hints:

- Each of the small villages—not counting the Roman fort—has a resource: Food, Wood, Gold, Stone, Villagers, or troops. Your Tarkans suggest what to do in each village to capture a resource.
- This is a raid—get what you can and get out! Destroying some of the buildings grants you resources, but it's not necessary to raze every enemy building.
- Notice the locations of resources. You might need them later.
- The Huns are still confined to the Castle Age.

Scout Reports:

- Attila's Huns (yellow) invade the Eastern Roman Empire with several Cavalry but no Villagers. They expect only token resistance from all of the villages.
- The exception is the Roman army (blue), which has a fortified base to the east. Do not attempt to invade it until you are prepared.
- The other villages might have Food, Wood, Gold, Stone, Villagers, or troops that you can use to challenge the Romans.

First Walkthrough: Town to Town

You begin this mission with two formations and a mandate to plunder the countryside before going up against the main Roman camp. Heed your calling and send one of your forces to the east and the other to the west to look for enemy villages. To the east, you run across the Goth village of Naissus, where you can pillage some Wood. Destroy the four Lumber Camps you find, and send your units back to the west to join the rest of your forces, which should have discovered the Franks town of Sofia.

At Sofia, a few Frankish Archers needle you until you smite them, after which you should pass the outlying buildings and bear down on the Sofia Town Center. Level it and you receive a cache of Food for your efforts. With your forces joined, head southwest toward the western corner of the map. When you come upon the Teuton city of Dyrrhachium, locate the Palisade that's protecting a Trebuchet and a company of Archers on the outskirts of town. Have your Tarkans break in and destroy the Trebuchet while your Cavalry Archers engage the enemy Archers.

> **Tip:** *Managing your wounded pays off big in this scenario. If you have badly wounded units, separate them before you go in harm's way. You'll soon be building a Castle where everyone can heal, so it's worth it to keep every unit alive that you can.*

You'll soon be informed that some comrades are being held in a nearby Castle. You also encounter an angry gaggle of Teuton Spearmen. Meet their advance with a hasty withdrawal to the west—don't trifle with Spearmen when you're sitting on a Horse.

Heading west, you come across the walls of the castle, which you should follow to the west, south, and then east. Circle the Castle to reveal your imprisoned comrades (as shown in Figure 7-5) as well as a flight of arrows from the Castle.

Quickly set your imprisoned brethren to hacking their way free while you send your main force east, out of range of the Teuton Castle.

When your main force clears the Castle's fire, have them bash their way into the Teuton town to join the escaped prisoners. Once inside, set your Tarkans to destroying the Town Center nearby, while your Cavalry Archers stand ready to fire on the Spearmen, which should arrive momentarily.

Figure 7-5   Free your imprisoned brethren immediately, and move them out of range of the Castle!

When you leave the Frankish fortress, set your Tarkans' stance to Stand Ground so that they attack only units you direct toward them. Move east; trail your Cavalry Archers behind a short distance to negate their extended line of sight and ability to fire at range. Locate the Byzantine city of Thessalonica, and proceed with care lest you overrun your objective and destroy what you came for.

Destroy all of the buildings at Thessalonica while you fight off a few Archers and an angry Monk. However, try to keep the number of Villagers you kill to a minimum because the survivors will be yours when the last building falls. If you leave the Byzantine Fishing Boats alone, you might reap one or two of them as well.

> **Tip:** *Bring your Cavalry Archers in only when there are no Villagers around, or they pick them off from range. Instead, use Tarkans to attack individual armed units when Villagers are visible or to run down fleeing units that might expose Villagers as they move. If you're careful, you should come away with plenty of workers to help build your new town.*

When the last Byzantine billet falls and the Villagers are yours, build a Town Center on the site of the razed city and start cranking out Villagers as fast as you can. To add Food to your stores, build farms immediately and keep producing workers. Whether or not you inherited any Fishing Boats, build a Dock nearby and take advantage of all those Byzantine Fishing Traps.

Send your healthiest troops east to look for the Byzantine city of Adrianople. When they arrive, have them take out the two Gold Mines on the western edge of the city, but watch for two Monks who try to stop them. When they have the Gold, return the troops to your town and prepare to defend it for a time.

By now, your Villagers should be harvesting the local herd of deer and you should have a Lumber Camp in operation. If you haven't done so, send a Villager to mine the Gold to your west and another to the Stone deposits north of the Teuton Castle. (Watch out for arrows; that Castle is still a threat!) For the time being, put a premium on gathering Stone because building a Castle is key to your defense.

When you have the resources, build an Archery Range and upgrade it, and supply more Cavalry Archers and a Blacksmith for Cavalry upgrades to your Tarkans. Build a Castle to heal your injured units and to enable the building of Tarkans and Petards.

By this time, the Romans notice your efforts and begin raiding your township, probably from the east. Resist the urge to do anything other than parry their blows—you're still too weak to prevail in a concerted attack. Put together a force of Petards at the Castle, and garrison them as you build them. When you have an imposing force, send the bulk of it, along with any siege engines you have, east and clear out Adrianople, which is probably teeming with Roman raiders. You don't want them hitting you from behind when you strike toward the Roman enclave, so make sure the area is clean.

Heal up, and add the rest of your forces (except the Petards). Push east and then north toward the Roman city. Take out anything and anyone that stands before you to clear the way for the Petards to follow in your wake. When your main body reaches the Roman moat, have it wait just out of range of the Roman Guard Towers while you send up your Petards en masse. Your presence draws attention, but the forces that come out to meet you expose themselves to your speed, so do your best to run them into the ground and catch them in crossfire.

When you have your Petards at hand, throw a couple of them at the main gate. (See Figure 7-6.) If it doesn't blow open completely, attack it next with Tarkans until you break through. Rush into the city with all of your forces, keeping the rest of your Petards close to the rear.

Figure 7-6   *When you're ready to blow the Roman gate, two or three Petards should do the job.*

Move everyone to the east away from the Roman Castle, and turn northeast, pushing on against all resistance until you come to the Town Center. Hit it with your Petards, and if it doesn't fall immediately throw your surviving Tarkans at it. When you destroy the building, the Roman will to fight crumbles as well.

Second Walkthrough: To the Swift Go the Spoils

Form your units into two groups—the first all Tarkans, the second Cavalry Archers—and head them southwest. Change the stance on both formations to Stand Ground, and follow the tree line you encounter to the southwest and then south. Ignore enemy units or buildings along the way, and keep moving. Follow the edge of the forest as it swings southeast; then head east past the Teutonic Mill

and Farms. As you move east, make sure your Cavalry Archers lag behind so that they don't open up on the Thessalonican Villagers, which are crucial to your plans.

Move the Tarkans ahead until they catch a glimpse of the Lumber Camp being worked by Byzantine Villagers from Thessalonica. (See Figure 7-7.) Then break off and head south-southeast to look for the town of Thessalonica itself.

When you find the Village, raze it, *but do not under any circumstances kill any Villagers!* A few Archers and a Monk attack you, but you should be able to absorb the damage while you move your formations in for the kill.

If you exercise great care, when Thessalonica falls, you find yourself in command of six Villagers. Have them build a Town Center on the spot, and while they're doing that, change the stance of your units to Defensive.

When the Town

Figure 7-7 *At the Lumber Camp, you should draw the Archers away and leave the Villagers alone!*

Center is done, round up every unit under your command—Villagers included—and send them east along the forest's edge. Follow the woods east, northeast, and then north, where you encounter the first Outposts of the Roman city.

Continue north until you see an opening into the forest marked with two orange torches. Enter the forest with all of your units; ignore any warning, and send a few Tarkans along to the end. You soon discover the grisly retreat of three Scythian Wild Women, who request six Villagers in exchange for their aid. (See Figure 7-8.) Make the deal!

Ride north and take possession of your new weapons, grouping your Wolves and Petards into separate bands. Head everybody back out of the forest and south toward the first Roman Outpost you saw; then scout ahead, to locate the southwestern gate.

Figure 7-8 *Meet the Wild Women's terms and you will soon have the resources you need.*

Send two Petards against the gate to blow it open, and rush in with your Wolves, using them to engage and harass any defensive forces. Follow up with the rest of your forces immediately, sheltering your Petards as much as possible with your mounted troops. Hang a quick right inside the gate; then march everyone northeast until you spot the Roman Town Center. Set your Petards against it, and blow it to smithereens!

Mission Three: The Walls of Constantinople

Objectives:

- Stockpile 10,000 Gold in tribute from the Romans.

Hints:

- Although your goal is to collect Gold, do not worry about spending it to train troops. Huns make money by extorting the Romans, not by conservation!
- Destroying Roman Town Centers, Docks, Markets, and similar buildings scares the Romans into paying. But despite their protests, do no cease until you have 10,000 Gold.
- You cannot merely trade resources for the Gold you need. Your objective is to exact a tribute from the Romans.
- The Huns might not go to the Imperial Age.

Scout Reports:

- The Huns (yellow) have a small town that they need to defend against early attacks from Marcianopolis (green).
- Marcianopolis does not have a strong army, but its town is walled, which can prevent an early Hunnic attack. After you breach the gates, however, the town should crumble.
- Initially, only a few towers defend Phillippopolis (red), but it trains an army of infantry and Light Cavalry.
- Constantinople (blue) is by far the greatest threat. The City's famous walls are hard to siege, but it is not necessary to do so. Extort money from the Romans and you will be victorious.

First Walkthrough: Scouring the Countryside

You must compel the Byzantines at Constantinople to pay you 10,000 Gold in tribute. Although a princely sum, this plan has a practical aspect because only one Gold deposit exists on the landscape, and taking it is not without risk. Early on, managing the Gold you *do* have is at least as important as fending off the Goth attacks, which, by the way, start immediately.

Send your Tarkans and your Monk north to fight off the Goth attack on your Mill. Kill the Men-at-Arms, but try to convert the Cavalry unit with your Monk before the Tarkans take it out. When you stem the attack, move your Monk in to heal your Tarkans, but don't let the Monk get in harm's way. Other Goth units are nearby, and more are on the way from Marcianopolis, to the east.

Begin building Villagers and more military units, including at least one Cavalry Scout. Send the Scout exploring in the mountains to the west to look for a Relic. After the Scout discovers it, and your Monk has your fighting force in good health, have some Villagers build a Monastery while your Monk retrieves the Relic.

> **Tip:** *Because of the premium on Gold, plan to build an early force of Spearmen, Skirmishers, and Cavalry, which do not require Gold to build.*

Clear out any remaining Goths in the field directly north and build a Lumber Camp there. Send Villagers to gather Wood and to farm around the Mill, and station your small army between them and the Goth attackers coming from Marcianopolis.

When the Relic is in the Monastery, you bring in a little extra Gold, so build another Monk, and an Archery Range for producing Skirmishers. Keep building Villagers, and put them to work to bring in the resources that are the basis for your fighting force. When in doubt, think, "Food! Wood! Food! Wood!"

By now the bow-happy Byzantines from the southwest will probably have made pests of themselves, but don't be lulled away by their probing attacks. Although you need to have some Skirmishers ready to drive them off if they attack in earnest, they won't attack in force any time soon.

When your troops have the mettle, and a couple of Monks to back them up, build a Siege Workshop and three Rams. When the Rams are ready to move, move your forces toward the Goth gate and send your Rams in to breach the wall. Take on any resistance you stir up, and keep the Rams in good shape with a Villager if you need to.

When you breach the Goth wall, rush in and start dismantling the city. Bash the Town Center with your Rams, and when it falls, you net a 3,000 Gold tribute from Constantinople. Each of the Docks you destroy nets you another 500 Gold.

With your tribute secure, send all of your forces to the southern side of your town in preparation for an advance on the Byzantine city of Phillippopolis in the southwest. (See Figure 7-9.) Although it has no protective walls, several armed towers guard Phillippopolis, and plenty of Archers and Pikemen greet you.

When your troops have healed, move everyone straight South toward an inlet; then wait momentarily to see if you can disrupt trade between Phillippopolis and Constantinople. If a Trade Cart comes by and you destroy it, you secure another 500 Gold in tribute.

When you're ready, advance on Phillippopolis. Send your Rams ahead to smash towers and buildings, and cover them with the ranged attacks of your Skirmishers. When you level the Town Center, you get another 3,000 Gold, and 500 each for destroying the Market and the Dock. (A second Relic is to the west, should you feel you need it.)

Figure 7-9   *Massing for attack against the Byzantines in the south. Note the squads of Skirmishers.*

Build a Dock by the shore, and upgrade to War Galleys and crank out two. When they're afloat, send them off to hunt down the two Trade Cogs from Constantinople that should be headed in your general direction. If you chase them into the inlet, they won't be able to escape the fire from your ships and shore forces. (See Figure 7-10). When the second Cog goes down, you net another 500 Gold and victory is at hand.

Figure 7-10   *Herding the two Roman Trade Cogs into this inlet makes sinking them a breeze.*

Second Walkthrough: Up Against the Wall

Although 10,000 Gold in tribute is nothing to sneeze at, a truly powerful army wouldn't let a trivial detail like double walls stand in the way of conquest. To tackle Constantinople, follow the initial steps in the first walkthrough, with the following changes:

- Destroy only the Town Centers in Marcianopolis and Philppopolis, not the Docks, Markets, or Trade Routes.
- Begin upgrading your units and building more and better forces from the get-go, and increase that build-up after you start bringing in Gold. (Having both Relics comes in handy now, so pick up both if you can.)
- Mine either the Stone at Marcianopolis or the larger Stone deposits south of your village. You'll build two Castles, so you'll need plenty of rock.

When you have the Stone, whip up a Castle in your hometown, not only to make it possible to build more of those bruising Tarkans, but also to compel Constantinople to cough up another 500 Gold. When you're pushing at your 75-unit limit, swing east from Phillippopolis and take out the Byzantine Monastery at the end of the inlet. Keep your eyes out for Monks nearby, and smash them at every opportunity—*short of getting drawn close to Constantinople's bristling walls.*

Next move your whole force north along the western edge of the city, within range of the Outposts outside Constantinople's walls. Knock the Outposts down as you go, fighting off any attacks from the city, but don't let yourself get drawn into a pitched battle. Keep moving north, cutting down the Outposts, until your full fighting force, including any new Tarkan replacements, is massed along the shore north of the city.

Build a Dock on the shore, and when you have enough Stone, build another Castle at the end of the paved brick leading out from Constantinople's northern gate. Stock the castle with Archers, Crossbowmen. or Elite Skirmishers, and station the remainder of your units in the lee of the Castle. (See Figure 7-11.)

Make an assault on the northern Guard Towers and the outer gate with your siege engines, making good tactical use of a Villager or two to return your catapults to full strength if they sustain damage. When the forces of Constantinople counterattack, fall back under the protection of your Castle and use ranged weapons to cut them down.

After you quell the counterattack, attack again. This time breach the second gate. Fall back again in the face of deter-

Figure 7-11 *Use Mangonels to breach the gates and a Castle and army to greet the Roman counterattack.*

mined counterattacks, and push into the city itself and take out a few important buildings. When you finally push close to the Byzantine Castle, you should reap another 1,000 Gold from the Byzantines, who hope that you will leave their Wonder alone. This should give you a good idea of how to get the remaining 10,000 in Gold.

At the Dock, upgrade to War Galleys, and build a fleet and sail it southeast along the city walls. When you get to the Sea Wall, breach it; take out the Fire Ships inside, and destroy the Dock (as shown in Figure 7-12), to net another 1,000 Gold. Build Transports and move the bulk of your forces ashore from the sea, and attack the Wonder from inside Constantinople's walls. When the Wonder falls, the Byzantines pay a 5,000 Gold tribute, which puts you over the top.

Figure 7-12 *Constantinople's defenses are weakest toward the sea, exposing its Wonder to a landing.*

Mission Four: A Barbarian Betrothal

Objectives:

- Defeat Orleans.
- Defeat Metz.
- Defeat Burgundy.

Hints:

- Your forces are scattered at the beginning. Look for a good place for an initial camp while you avoid Wolves. In the dead of winter, forage sites are hard to come by, but you can find hungry deer.
- You cannot match the Frankish technology, but you do have the strength of numbers. Unleash the horde upon the cities of Gaul!

Scout Reports:

- After invading Gaul, the Huns (yellow) begin scattered. They must regroup but not stumble too close to Burgundy (purple) in the south, Metz (red) to the north, or the great city of Orleans (cyan) to the northwest.
- Burgundy trains Archers, Rams, and infantry but is not well defended and might fall to an early attack. You can intimidate the Burgundians easily and might even be able to persuade them to join the Hunnic cause.
- Metz makes up for Burgundy's weakness with an army of Knights and Throwing Axemen. The Castle and proximity to Orleans offers Burgundy some defense.
- Orleans is a walled city protected by Towers and Castles. Its army of Spearmen, Knights, and Monks might prove a challenge for the Huns.
- Scouts also report that the Western Roman Empire is sending Aetius's army to reinforce Gaul. The Romans have no town in the area, but their Legions and Cataphracts could strike at any time.

First Walkthrough: Division by Diplomacy

To begin, round up your dispersed Villagers and send them to the eastern corner of the map, but don't let them travel through uncharted territory alone. A Wolf or two might take more than a liking, so have your Scout Cavalry give safe passage through the wilds.

After your Scout Cavalry sees your Villagers safely to the site of your new village, send them off to get a quick look around. While they're scouting, have your Villagers build a Town Center between the Gold and Stone deposits (as shown in Figure 7-13), and start gathering Stone, Gold, and Wood. Because few ready food sources are available in the depths of winter, it's not too early to emphasize Food production.

For now, your only Food expense should be building Villagers to bring in more resources, especially more Food. Still, don't fixate on grub alone. You need plenty of Stone to build a Castle.

> **Tip:** When you need defensive units, you can get Spearmen, Archers, and their upgrades for Wood and Gold, which allows you to use your Food to keep adding Villagers at a blistering pace. Even better, you recover your expenses more quickly that way.

Scout the terrain to the near north, west, and south to get an idea of how you can take advantage of natural features to aid the defense of your growing community. Also note any available resources

that might be worth penning in when you build defensive walls so that you won't have to risk life and limb to stay solvent.

When you have the resources, build an Archery Range, a Monastery, and a Siege Workshop, in that order. Upgrade your archery units at the Archer Range; build a Monk at the Monastery for healing, and build the Siege Workshop in the short term to allow you to advance to the Imperial Age. Advance as soon as you can.

Keep harvesting resources, generating

Figure 7-13 *Site your Town Center in the east, surrounded by resources, and crank out the Villagers!*

Food, and building a solid workforce to supply you when you're in the thick of battle. Use a Villager or two to close your perimeter with Stone Walls, and take advantage of the cliffs that surround you. Build a few Guard Towers near the walls to extend your line of sight, and garrison an Archer or two inside if you want. Try to keep at least 500 Gold in the bank at all times because the Burgundians make an offer you

want to be able to accept. When they do make contact, they promise allegiance in exchange for a tribute of 500 Gold and the building of a Castle in their city to help with defenses. Accept their offer and follow their instructions, and soon you have one less foe and a well-protected left flank.

Although the tribute hurts your Gold reserves, the Market you build allows you to recover the loss via trade with Burgundy. Upgrade the Market, get your Trade Carts moving, and reap the rewards of your diplomacy.

Note: *As soon as you send the tribute, an onscreen message notifies you that you have ten minutes in which to build the Castle on the specified site. To meet this schedule, refrain from making the tribute until you have sufficient Villagers and Stone to build the Castle in short order. Also, provide an escort when your Villagers make the journey south so that a chance enemy patrol doesn't ruin your plans.*

Concentrate now on building and upgrading your armed forces. Upgrade to Elite Tarkans at your Castle in Burgundy, build a Barracks if you don't already have one, and upgrade Spearmen to Halberdiers. Build a Blacksmith, and upgrade there as well. When you have a large and powerful force—Elite Tarkans, Heavy Cavalry Archers, Elite Skirmishers, Halberdiers, Mangonels, and a Monk or two—move it toward the northeast, past the large deposit of Gold. Stay in tight formation, try to avoid detection, and change your stance so that your units don't chase after small patrols or sentries.

When you pass the end of the frozen river, turn toward the northwest and probe ahead to look for the Market at Metz. When you find it, skirt around it to the east and north; move your forces into position opposite the Market from the Castle, which is to the southwest. Make sure your formation is solid, with units facing southwest toward the market, and then open up and let the Market have it *with your ranged weapons only*!

Tip: *Your Halberdiers and Tarkans should be in front, acting like a wall against which the counterattacking Frankish defenses crash while your Skirmishers, Cavalry Archers, and Crossbowmen cut them down.*

While you're attacking the Metz Market, chopping up the units that rush to meet you and probing ahead to lure still more defenders to their doom, build a second small force at your Castle centered around Tarkans and Trebuchets. When it's ready to roll, send it up in the traces of your first formation, moving the Trebuchets in behind your line. If you haven't leveled the Market yet—or, more likely, if you have and it's being rebuilt nearby—have your Trebuchets lay it to waste.

Without changing the dynamic between your forces, advance them until your Trebuchets can draw a bead on the Castle. Take out the Castle, and continue to use your defensive wall to cut any attacking enemy forces before they draw near. When the Castle falls, move again but only far enough to take the Town Center. When *it* falls, Metz is yours.

Note: *A group of Rams is a powerful, destructive force made all the more so by the inclusion of a group of Halberdiers inside. Weakest against heavy cavalry, an empty Ram simply collapses when it is destroyed, but a well-stocked Ram unleashes exactly the right units to defeat the attacking foe. Fill all your Rams with infantry!*

Continue your slow advance toward Orleans while you file another large force of combined arms from Skirmishers to Trebuchets. Build plenty of Halberdiers, and consider upgrading to Siege Rams and using them to carry some of your infantry. Send this second force west across the bridge in the center of the map, massing it just out of range of the Castle in southern Orleans.

While your second force is coming into play toward the south, move your northern army slowly toward Orleans to look for a second, more northerly Castle. Attack it as you did the Castle at Metz to take it out, and remove the Guard Towers nearby as well. Overrun the southern Castle with your second force, and converge on the main gate.

Move into Orleans in a slow, determined advance. Keep the enemy in front of you, and use the Trebuchets and any other siege engines to take out the offensive buildings and enemy artillery you encounter. Before you invade the Orleans Town Center, pause and regroup, making sure your units are in tight formations.

When the Town Center of Orleans falls, Roman troops flood up from the south and deliver a heavy blow. You *must* absorb this attack! Target your Trebuchets and siege engines on the path they're using to soften them up before

they come into play toward
your Archers and Skir-
mishers. Don't break
ranks, even if you are
overrun! If you can
withstand the Roman
assault and continued
attacks by the forces of
Orleans, you can accel-
erate your advance and
destroy all the offen-
sive buildings in the
city. When the city
center is finally clear,
pushing through the
gate to the north (as
shown in Figure 7-14)
brings you face to face
with the last of the en-
emy resistance. When
the landscape is in
ruin, victory is at hand.

Figure 7-14   *The remaining assets of Orleans lie beyond, but you have the force to meet them.*

Second Walkthrough: The Way of the Hun

Sometimes it's more satisfying to destroy everything in your path. Send your Scout Cavalry quickly to the south to scout the Frankish town of Burgundy. Harass the Villagers you find there, and scope out the various avenues that give the Franks access your eastern outpost. Your immediate goals are to reveal the lay of the land and to slow the Franks as much as possible, but don't get any units killed in the process.

Gold will be your least plentiful resource for a while, but Food and Wood you'll have aplenty, so field your early forces accordingly. Build an Archery Range, upgrade to Elite Skirmishers, and crank them out by the dozen. Build a Blacksmith, and upgrade your Archer's skills when you can. Build your Town Center between the Gold and Stone deposits you find in the east, and begin mining Stone for a Castle. Build more Villagers, and set them to work farming. When you have the Food, build more Villagers to chop Wood and mine Gold. Upgrade your farms, and keep adding more so that you can build more Villagers.

When your Scout Cavalry exposes the three forest paths leading from Burgundy to the open field south of your encampment, run some Villagers down there and block those paths with Stone Walls. Build one wall very close to Burgundy if possible so that the Franks will tackle it head on, and then back that wall up with one or two more. It won't stop them, but it will slow them and keep them busy for a while. (See Figure 7-15.)

Figure 7-15 *For the time being, use Stone Walls to keep Burgundy busy and at arm's reach.*

When the harassing attacks against your town from Orleans, Metz, and Burgundy increase, build a Castle as a defensive anchor just west of your Town Center. Stock the Castle with a few Archers and a bunch of Skirmishers, and build a Barracks and upgrade to Halberdiers, fielding a dozen or so when you can.

Build some Light Cavalry, Tarkans, and a Trebuchet or two, and then add your Skirmishers and Halberdiers and head south to take on the

Burgundians. If you're fortunate, you'll catch them behind one of your walls, but in any case, you should be able to fight past them and make your way toward their city. If they offer you an alliance in exchange for Gold, ignore their entreaty and pound away. From here on out, try to keep forces in the field and stay on the offensive against Burgundy. The bad news is that allied units from Metz and Orleans come to their aid, but the good news is that they launch few attacks against your city.

As you attack, keep searching for new buildings the Burgundians have erected to keep their civilization alive, particularly toward the central bridge over the river. Stay on their heels, and try to wipe them out as soon as possible. While doing so, send Scouts into the south and west to look for Gold deposits to mine. The Burgundian territory is a rich one, which is a good reason to conquer it quickly.

When Burgundy falls, mine all the Gold you can. For protection, add a few defensive units or structures near your mines. The territory you hold is vast, and enemy units will surely make forays against you that you might not be able to defeat in time. Use your Gold to upgrade your units and to replenish your army. At the same time, push west along the southern side of the river until you arrive at your end of the bridges south of Orleans. When you have sufficient forces in place, cross the bridges until you attract the attention of the forces of Orleans, and lure them to their doom. Repeat until you clear the two bridges for crossing.

Have several Villagers begin building a second town south of the southern bridge near the Stone deposits, and mine more Stone if you need it to build a second Castle. Build the Castle at your end of the bridge (as shown in Figure 7-16) for defense and to increase your line of sight, and garrison ranged units. Build a Barracks and crank out Halberdiers.

Figure 7-16   *Your second Castle draws attention from Orleans, depleting the city's defenses.*

When you're ready, push north toward Orleans and take out the Town Center. In response, the Roman army streams toward Orleans, primarily along the northern side of the river, but at times right past or through your new town. Use your position to cut any Roman units down to size before they reinforce Orleans.

Attack the Romans relentlessly until you finish them off, and then send heavy armies against the southern flank of Orleans and the northern flank of Metz. Hammer at the two cities with Rams and Trebuchets to take down walls and Castles, and flood the battlefield with Halberdiers to counter the enemy cavalry. Keep the pressure on and destroy the enemy's ability to rebuild, and soon the lands will fall silent.

Mission Five: The Catalaunian Fields

Objectives:

- Defeat the Romans, Alans, and Visigoths.

Hints:

- This battle plays like a death match. Prepare for attack almost immediately, but don't forget to collect resources to replenish your losses.

Scout Reports:

- The Huns (yellow) and their allies, the Ostrogoths (red), occupy the right side of the battlefield.
- The Romans (blue) and their allies, the Visigoths (green) and Alans (cyan), are drawn up across the creek on the left side of the battlefield.
- The embattled Franks (gray) get caught in the middle of the battle and are soon defeated. Their fate is not the Huns' concern.
- Among your enemies, the Romans are the most dangerous. Their infantry, Cataphracts, and siege weapons initially try to hit the Ostrogoths on the Huns' flank. The Visigoths train Huskarls and some Cavalry, whereas the Alans are composed mostly of Spearmen and Archers.

First Walkthrough: The Sweep

Although you start with a pile of resources, so do your enemies. You can expect enemy assaults to come your way by the time you send your first Villagers forth.

Your early objective is to build a defense that can take the oncoming assaults and give you time to build a dominant force of your own. To that end, build a Town Center near the two torches just north of you; situate your building between the Gold and Stone deposits nearby. Herd sheep toward the Town Center for slaughter, and make plans for gathering other resources as well. Although you're flush, you'll soon wish you had twice as many resources on hand.

Build plenty of Villagers and set some of them to work building a Castle just west of your Town Center. Build an Archery Range, a Blacksmith, and more Villagers to help with the buildings. When that's done, send the Villagers to replenish the resources you used, and stock your Castle with upgraded ranged units.

About now, the Romans show up and do some damage, their aim being to slow down your budding Hun community. If you attack carefully with your Tarkans, keeping them in range of the hail of arrows from the Castle, you should be able to defeat the attack without losing a unit. Build a Monastery and a Monk to help heal units even if you send some units to the Castle. You'll need mobile medics soon enough anyway.

In the wake of the Roman assault, build a Stone Wall from the forest in the south out around your Castle and up toward your ally in the north. Don't bother closing the wall off in the north yet because that cuts off your Villagers from your Castle's defenses. The goal is to block the approach of the Visigoths from the south.

When the Villagers are done with the Stone Wall, have them gather resources of all kinds, including more Stone, and advance your civilization to the Imperial Age. Upgrade to Elite Tarkans and Heavy Cavalry Archers with Parthian Tactics, and plan to make a horde of each. They'll be the mainstay of your assault force and act as a defensive screen for the Trebuchets you later use to flatten the opposition.

Build Tarkans and Cavalry Archers in a one to two ratio, forming them into two combined units with a wall of Tarkans in the front and two rows of Cavalry Archers to the rear. Because you'll be sending these mounts afield, build a Siege Workshop and then build some Mangonels and Scorpions to help defend your city when they're gone.

When your two formations are ready, send them south across the twin bridges to the outskirts of the Visigoth village. Change to a less-aggressive stance so that your forces won't charge into harm's way; then probe slowly, keeping the formations close together. As you enter the Visigoth

> **Tip:** _At your Castle, if you build Conscription, you'll get a 33 percent boost in the rate at which your key units are built. Build Conscription early!_

> **Tip:** _Don't be tempted to bog down these mounted formations with any Monks or other slow-moving units. Not only are your formations potent, they're fast and maneuverable, and you need to keep them that way._

1939 3554 3600 1055 96/100 Imperial Age

Figure 7-17 *The Visigoths are little match for your Heavy Cavalry Archers and Tarkans.*

town, take advantage of the Cavalry Archers' range and firepower, using your Tarkans to hold any attacking units while the Archers stick them. (See Figure 7-17.)

While you're softening up the Visigoths, build a third formation centered around three Trebuchets. Add a few Scorpions or Mangonels, a few Monks, and some Tarkans and Heavy Cavalry Archers as defensive escorts. This heavy-hitting formation moves slowly, so keep it to the rear of your two mounted brigades.

When you're ready and Visigoth resistance has fallen off, send the Trebuchets to level the town. Take your time, stay alert for flanking attacks from the Romans, and don't leave until the Visigoths have announced that they are through. Turn northwest, sending one fast column ahead to clear the way, and advance to an abandoned Frankish town. To the northeast, the Viking city of Alans is your next objective, but don't head straight up the road to the north. Instead, push into the shallows to the northwest and attack there, keeping your trebuchets protected on all sides.

Resistance is stronger at Alans, but the plan is the same. Prompt the Vikings to counterattack, and whittle them down while your Trebuchets pound away. Be on guard for crossfire from the Viking Castles and Town Centers, but don't be afraid to press the advantage when you have it. In short order, you should be able to destroy Alans.

Tip: *As you move into and then through the Viking city, be careful not to let your Trebuchets attack too far ahead. The Roman city borders Alans, and accidentally nicking a Roman building unleashes a furious retort.*

Before you tangle with the Roman war machine, you should be in excellent health and you should bolster your army

with a strong formation of Halberdiers. When you attack the Romans, they reply with a heavy force, led by extremely tough Elite Cataphracts, and you cannot be too ready to meet this charge. (See Figure 7-18.)

Figure 7-18   *When the Romans respond to your assault on their city, the fields run red with blood.*

In the face of overwhelming odds, you should abandon your Trebuchets and use your mobility to advantage. Keep pressing the attack, however, and if you need a second army, have it ready before your first is vanquished. The Romans fight until you have gutted their economy and hacked their army to pieces, at which point you can train your Trebuchets on their hollow assets and deliver them to Caesar.

Second Walkthrough: Arm in Arm

Although you face three foes, the Romans alone are your nemesis, and they should rightly incur your wrath. Although you'll have to protect yourself against assaults from all three enemies, the best way to keep the Romans off balance is to hit them first and hit them often.

The immediate objectives are ramping up your Food and Wood production and fielding and upgrading a defensive force of Archers, Skirmishers, and Spearmen. Send your Villagers and sheep east, and build a Town Center just northeast of the Forage Bushes you find there. Start building fifteen Villagers while your original three build a Blacksmith, Barracks, and Archery Range.

Send your Tarkans and Scout to look around, particularly to the west and south. When you spot the two bridges to the south, scout around on your side of the river but don't cross over into Visigoth territory: they visit you soon enough as it is. Note also the areas scouted by your Ostrogoth ally to the north, including the shallows in the north that take you into Roman-held lands.

Quickly build up your city and your defensive units, and upgrade every chance you get. Soon you should have at least fifty units guarding your village, and twenty Villagers supporting it. By this time, you'll have already endured several attacks from the Visigoths in the south and you should have some idea of what you need to have in place to meet these recurrent threats.

Add a Monastery and a Monk or two to keep your defensive forces healthy after each tilt, and then build a Castle just to the north between the two Gold deposits and the Stone. Stock the Castle with Archers, but leave room for wounded defenders to pile in as well. Send Villagers to mine the Gold and Stone, and if you haven't already, advance to the Imperial Age as soon as possible.

Build a second force of mixed arms, and station them defensively along the road to the southwest of the Castle. Most of the western attacks come from that direction, although you need to keep a lookout for Roman offensives from the north—some of which can be considerable. When you've used about eighty of your maximum one hundred units, build twenty Tarkans and upgrade to Elite Tarkans if you haven't already done so. Send this force north into Ostrogoth territory and then northwest, crossing into Roman territory via the shallows north of the blown bridge.

Sweep into the Roman lands and destroy any outlying buildings you find there. Take on a few Cataphracts if you have the health, but when you sustain wounds, beat a hasty retreat to the Ostrogoth Castle!

While you're healing at the Ostrogoth's Castle, replace any Tarkans you lost and continue upgrading your abilities and gathering resources. To increase your Gold receipts, build a Market and trade with the Ostrogoths—provided the Romans haven't flattened their Market.

Tip: *Not only is the Ostrogoth Castle closer, but you gain two distinct advantages by going there instead of heading home. First, any pursuing Roman forces will be met by the Ostrogoths themselves, saving wear and tear on your army. Second, you can keep your own Castle stocked with Archers, as well as keep it available for healing and protecting your defenders and miners.*

Make another raid or two to clear any Roman buildings and forces between the , end of the shallows and the forest to the northwest. While doing so, scout the Roman rear for a complex containing several Castles, a number of Guard Towers, and a Town Center. (See Figure 7-19.) When you find it, take out a Guard Tower or two to rile the Romans, and then head back to the Ostrogoth Castle.

From here on out, replace any units you lose on your raids or while defending your city with more powerful forces, including Rams and Trebuchets. Send these with your Tarkans each time they plunder the Roman countryside, and do as much damage as possible before you have to withdraw your wounded mounts. You lose your heavy machinery, but you do irreparable damage to the Romans in the process.

If you can, destroy a Castle with one raid and a Town Center and Barracks with another. This strategy puts a heavy load on the Roman economy and severely tests the Roman defenses. When Roman resistance begins to wane, you see fewer Cataphracts and more infantry, which should be your signal to step up attacks.

When the Romans are on their heels, build a large force of Tarkans and a few Trebuchets and hit the city as hard as possible. Use the Tarkans to run down any enemy forces trying to get to the Trebuchets while you turn the artillery loose on buildings and towers. Soon, in almost a single moment, the Roman resistance fails, and from then on you can pound your way through the countryside, overrunning and wiping out everything in your path (as shown in Figure 7-20), including the Vikings and Visigoths.

Figure 7-19 *In quick-hitting raids, a band of Tarkans can do extensive damage to the Roman city.*

Figure 7-20 *Having vanquished the Romans, a band of Tarkans plunders the Viking town of Alans.*

Mission Six: The Fall of Rome

Objectives:

- Defeat Milan, Padua, Verona, and Aquileia so that you can parlay with Rome.
- Attila must survive.

Hints:

- Do not attack the city of Rome. It's not a threat, and you need to leave someone to surrender to you.
- The Hun unique technology, Atheism, is useful if your opponent attempts a Relic or Wonder victory.
- Do not send all of your troops on the offensive if you lack sufficient resources to defend your town.
- When you do go on the offensive, make sure you have many fully upgraded units because your enemies will work together to stop you.

Scout Reports:

- The Huns (yellow) begin with ample resources in the foothills of the Alps. Below lie the well-defended city states of Northern Italy.
- Milan (green) has an aggressive army that might seek you out if you take too long to go on the offensive. Milan trains Knights and Archers and has a small navy.
- Padua (purple), which is known for its Archers and siege weapons, also lies to the north and might attack early.
- In the northern marshes lies Aquileia (red), which has few soldiers initially, but can eventually field Knights, Spearmen, and Scorpions.
- As the Huns advance through Italy, they eventually come into contact with Verona (orange), whose Knights, Archers, and Throwing Axemen offer the final defense of the Roman Empire.
- Rome itself (blue) lost most of its forces fighting the Huns in Gaul. After the Huns defeat the other cities, they can walk into Rome and proclaim themselves the new heirs to the Empire.

First Walkthrough: The Way of the Wonders

In your final battle, you face a gauntlet of aggressors and the arduous task of compelling each to yield in turn. Although you begin with ample resources, the enemy tasks you to poverty if you're not careful and the road to Rome becomes the road to ruin.

Your initial position is vulnerable from three directions: northeast, southwest, and southeast. Send Villagers to the northeast and southwest and have them build Stone Walls, closing off those avenues of approach. Also, site your walls a fair distance from your Town Center so that enemy Trebuchets can't park outside and shell your town.

Build an Archery Range and Blacksmith immediately, and make every upgrade you can at the Blacksmith. Even if you deplete your Gold reserves, you *must* strengthen the units you have or they will not survive the first few skirmishes. Upgrade, too, at

> **Tip:** *Situate* everything *you build to the north of the Town Center. A notch in the mountains to your south allows the enemy Trebuchet to fire from close range.*

the Archery Range, and build a bunch of Skirmishers: they are cheap, effective, and they don't require Gold. Build Villagers for Food and Wood, and add more as time passes.

Your first tactical objective is simply to survive the initial Teutonic attack from Milan, to your south. When they show up—and it will be soon—do not take them lightly or attack them indiscriminately. Keep your Tarkans up front and your Cavalry Archers in the rear, and use garrisoned Villagers to add fire from the Town Center if necessary.

As soon as you weather the assault from Milan, bolt into the south with your Tarkans and search for Trebuchets and Siege Engines, which are drawing near. The Teutons build these horrors by the minute, and you need to make frequent patrols into no-man's-land to keep them from devastating your position.

Build a Monastery and a Monk to heal up your wounded units, but don't rest. The forces of Aquileia to your north are probably on their way, circling around your wall to attack from the east. Clear the area to your south again with a quick sweep, and head back to town lest you be caught with your guard down.

If you've been scouting, you might have found a huge Gold deposit to the southwest of your western wall. After you survive the first few attacks, build a gate in that wall and send four Villagers down to mine that Gold.

> **Tip:** *Don't defend the Villagers or you'll increase the chance that they will be detected. Instead, keep probing and attacking the Teutons from the gap southeast of your Town Center, which keeps the Teuton forces headed in that direction.*

When a steady supply of Gold is coming in and you've checked that no Teuton forces are bearing down on you, send your Trebuchets and the bulk of your forces straight south to attack the Teuton Castle south of the Mill. Shell the Castle and destroy it if you can, but bug out when the Teutons deploy their own Trebuchets. It's not important that the Castle fall, just that you keep things stirred up and the Teutons on the offensive.

After you survive the counterattack of the enraged Teutons, heal up quickly and build a Castle to the west of your Town Center, well back from your defensive wall. Upgrade your Tarkans to Elite Tarkans; research Atheism to slow down your enemy's Wonders—at least one of which will already be underway—and build Trebuchets to replace or augment your original force.

When you have at least four Trebuchets and healthy forces, attack the Teuton Castle again; this time destroy it. When it falls, retreat to heal, resume your patrols, and send the bulk of the force back out the gate in the southwest. Head your army south, and destroy the two Siege Workshops inside Milan's wall. (See Figure 7-21.)

After you've made a dent in Milan, your job is to keep hitting it until it submits. Until then be ready for Siege Engines and Trebuchets to be on your heals at every step, and don't stop patrolling the plains and foothills north of the city. If you find any heavy artillery, use your Tarkans to smash it while you use your own Trebuchets to breach the western walls of the city. You must destroy two more Castles inside.

Figure 7-21   *Take out the two Siege Workshops in western Milan, and Onager production ceases.*

When Milan is about finished, you should already be building new forces and setting your sights on the Britains at Padua, directly to your east. If they do not yet have a Wonder complete, they will in mere moments, so ready your charge.

When ready, head your shock troops southeast, turn northeast, and attack Padua at the southwestern

gate. As with Milan, hit the city hard; shell a Siege Workshop or two, and withdraw when the Paduans counterattack in force. Again, the objective with the first attack is not to destroy the Wonder unless you're really running out of time. Instead, lure the enemy into the open, and cut them to pieces. When you've weathered the Paduan counterattack and healed up, head back to Padua and work your way around to the

> **Note:** *It's possible that Verona's Wonder might become the more pressing threat. If so, attack Verona first as outlined in the coming discussion, and then come back and hit Padua where it hurts. You need different troops for each city, so prepare accordingly!*

southern wall of the city. Attack the Wonder from there with your Trebuchets, but be on the watch for attacks from Verona to your southeast.

After you destroy the Paduan Wonder, fall back to your Town Center, regroup, and attack the city from the north; level it step by step. If you haven't upgraded your Rams to Siege Rams, do so and turn them loose within the city. Their Archers' arrows cause little damage, and you can use your mounted units to keep infantry and Siege Engines in check while the Rams wreak havoc.

Despite the pleasure of the task, you might have to break off your decimation of Padua if the Wonder at Verona is too far advanced. In any case, rebuild any depleted forces with an assault there in mind, and plan on completing the job in one

trip. Verona is a long march, and you won't have time to regroup for a second attack at your village.

When you make your move on Verona, harass the city from the southwest while you move your heavy arms and the bulk of your forces into position in the northeast. Four or five Trebuchets firing at once should take the Wonder down, as long as you protect them with other units until the deed is done. (See Figure 7-22.)

Figure 7-22   *A group of Trebuchets outside this gate quickly collapse the Veronese Wonder.*

After you collapse Verona's Wonder, you'll be pretty beat up, and foremost in your mind should be Attila's safety. No matter how many units remain, send Attila home to recover while you send the rest of your units north toward Padua. Have your new units, which you should have been building as your forces fell at Verona, meet your returning warrior, and rout whatever is left of the Paduan defenses.

Note: *You may never get a capitulation from Padua, even after the city has been leveled. When you lay siege to Verona, however, the mystery should be resolved.*

When you've destroyed what's left of Padua and defeated any counterattacks from Verona, set your sights on Aquileia in the north. You should be close to your maximum number of units by now, and their skills should be upgraded completely.

Note: *If you run out of Gold, look around in the south, near the shore. You might have to run off a few Veronese Villagers, but there's plenty to be had after you do.*

To crush Aquileia in a vise, send Trebuchets and Skirmishers north through your Stone Wall in the northeast, and have them rain death upon the city from the foothills above. From Padua, send your Cavalry and Tarkans to crush any Siege Engines and infantry, and then follow up with foot soldiers for mopping up. Aquileia will soon relent.

When Aquileia has fallen, you have only Verona to smite. Build a force of uncompromising size and strength, and ride boldly to the front gate and begin hammering away. Although resistance is stiff, your Hunnic forces will not be denied. After a heated battle, Verona submits to your will and Rome begs for mercy.

Second Walkthrough: Gate Crashing

Send your Villagers to build Stone Walls to the northeast, east, and south. Leave the southwest open, and prepare to defend there against attacks from every foe. Build ten more Villagers while you're building your walls, and put them to work erecting a Blacksmith, Lumber Camp, and Stable. Build a Tower or two inside your eastern wall to increase your line of sight.

Tip: *You'll want your walls far enough from your Village that a Trebuchet can't hit anything important from outside, but don't build your eastern wall too close to Padua. If you do, the Paduan army will feel obligated to knock it down.*

Get your Wood and Food production going full bore, and upgrade to Hussars and build a bunch of them. Upgrade to Plate Barding Armor and Blast Furnace at the Blacksmith to toughen up the mounts you already have, and get ready for a small but very tough column headed your way from Milan.

After you fight off the first attack, send Villagers to the Gold deposits in the hills to the southwest and begin mining them for all you're worth. You're going to be burning through Gold pretty soon, so stocking up and keeping it coming are important.

At the same time, send your Trebuchets and mounts south from the open gap, and have them take out the two Siege Workshops inside the walls of western Milan. As soon as they're gone, pack up and get out, and sweep the area with your Tarkans to look for any Milanese Onagers and Trebuchets that might have come out to play.

After you deal with any counterattacks, head home and build a Monastery and Monk to heal up your units. Build an Archery Range and Barracks, and crank out Skirmishers and Pikemen by the dozen. Station them close to the eastern edge of the gap, where enemy forces hug the foothills as they head for your town. At the Stable, upgrade to Paladins and start building them as well. You're going to need them to take care of heavy-hitting enemy Cavalry while your Tarkans do damage to enemy structures, so make sure you build enough to do the job. Also upgrade to Parthian Tactics and Heavy Cavalry Archers, and begin building them, too.

Send your Trebuchets back down to Milan with your Tarkans and Heavy Cavalry Archers, and take out some of the Guard Towers in the western part of the city. Blast a hole in the city wall if you can, but pack up and get out if enemy Trebuchets appear. Use your Tarkans to take them out while you repair any damage to your own Trebuchets.

> **Tip:** *If you lose your Trebuchets, build a Siege Workshop and go with Rams instead of building a Castle for more Trebuchets. When they don't have to deal with Onagers, Rams can do plenty of damage on their own and even more if you give them support.*

At some point, the Veronese and the Aquileians will send forces against you, and they might show up at the same time. Because they tend not to use Trebuchets early and they don't favor Onagers, you should be able to fight these forces off with a solid line of Pikemen backed by Skirmishers and Hussars.

During the next lull, send a strong force against Milan to take down the two Castles by the coast. (See Figure 7-23.) Gut the western end of town, and slip back outside the walls and around to the east demolish the Castle there as well. Finally, bash your way into the eastern end of town and destroy the Town Center and anything else to force Milanese to surrender.

When Milan falls, you should commit more Villagers to mining Gold and building a Castle near the open gap to your town. Upgrade to Elite Tarkans, and begin cranking Tarkans out by the tens, if not twenties. Build as many of your

Figure 7-23 *Two of the three Milanese Castles are along the coast and guarded by Fire Ships.*

most powerful mounts as you can, until you are close to your maximum allotted number of units, and then check the status of the enemy Wonders.

Either Padua or Verona come close to defeating you with a Wonder victory and might already be within a hundred years of doing so. Take a good look at the Wonder that is the most pressing threat, pick out a gate or wall that looks handy, and ride your entire mounted force of Paladins, Tarkans, Heavy Cavalry Archers, and Hussars to that point. When you arrive at the objective, have the Tarkans bash in a wall or gate and flood your forces inside. (See Figure 7-24.) While the Tarkans destroy the Wonder, have your Paladins deal with enemy Heavy Cavalry and siege weapons and have the Hussars and Cavalry Archers pick off infantry trying to attack the Tarkans. Keep attacking the Wonder until it falls; then leave the city immediately, and head back home to heal.

In all likelihood, you'll suffer serious casualties during your attack, so you should be building new units as the others fall in battle. When you have a second force in strength, send it against the next most advanced Wonder and repeat the attack and level it. Return this force to heal as well, and while doing so, begin to build Siege Rams and Trebuchets for doing lasting damage to the cities themselves.

Note: *You might be tempted to have your Tarkans slip through an open gate when the enemy comes out to meet your attack. Don't do it! You'll end up with your Tarkans inside and undefended. Worse, if they do manage to destroy the Wonder, they'll be so beat up they won't be able to get back out again. Make your own breach! You'll be sure you can escape, plus you'll have a way in for your next attack on the city.*

From here on out, you should send your Tarkan horde against any other Wonders that become a real threat—Aquileia is probably next—but spend most of your resources on a large force of combined arms geared toward taking down each city in turn. Because the Paduans are not particularly aggressive, you might want to hit Verona first, which would also let you take control of any Gold that remains in the deposits near the city, as well as the Gold reserves along the shore in the south near Rome.

Figure 7-24 *Have your Tarkans bash their way in so that you can be sure they'll be able to get out.*

Chapter Eight

THE EL CID CAMPAIGN

Rodrigo Diaz, or El Cid, was considered by some to be the greatest man who ever lived. The Cid was a knight and loyal vassal of one of the old kings of Spain. When the king died, the kingdom was divided between his two sons, Alfonso and Sancho.

King Sancho ruled Castille, an area named for the many castles that protected its borders, while King Alfonso ruled Leon. Alfonso unabashedly worked to become the king of all of Christian Spain, trying at every turn to depose his own brother, Sancho. This animosity soon led to war between the two sides, and The Cid was caught in the middle.

The Cid was loyal to King Sancho, but soon came under the rule of King Alfonso upon Sancho's death. Falling under the rule of a sworn enemy was a fate he accepted (as was his duty), but the animosity did not die with his pledge of allegiance. Indeed, King Alfonso was to exile The Cid, a move which ultimately led The Cid to unite both Moors and Christians in a common cause.

Mission One: Brother Against Brother

Objectives:

- Become King Sancho's Champion in a trial by combat.
- El Cid must survive.
- Take command of the Castillian army in order to capture King Sancho's conniving, ambitious brother, King Alfonso. Alfonso's Castle lies to the northwest, across the river.
- El Cid himself must bring the captured King Alfonso to King Sancho's tournament grounds.

Hints:

- Some of the folk of Castille may pledge themselves or their homes to the charismatic El Cid when they see him or his soldiers.
- Most of the Stone in Castille has already been quarried for its namesake castles. Almost all of the Stone that remains in the area is in the territory of King Alfonso.
- El Cid cannot yet advance to the Imperial Age.

Scout Reports:

- El Cid (red) starts alone and can only gain troops if they are granted by King Sancho.
- Sancho's subjects (yellow) are loyal to Sancho and friendly with The Cid; they might prove helpful.
- King Alfonso (blue) is your enemy. He has a well-fortified city. Your initial forces can probably damage his city, but it's likely you'll need to train some reinforcements, particularly siege weapons, to destroy his Castle. The border between Golpejera to the north and the Castillian border Castles to the south should have ample space and resources.
- Alfonso trains Knights and Pikemen, so guard your cavalry with Pikemen of your own.

First Walkthrough: Golpejera by Siege

As this mission begins you must first defeat two of King Sancho's champions in the tournament ring—first a Swordsman, and then a mounted knight. Both of these challenges will be met without any worry that El Cid will perish, so don't spend any time fretting over strategies.

Tip: *If you wait too long to grab a Horse from the stables (after the first tournament), you'll have to fight King Sancho's Knight on foot! Although this sounds daunting, you can emerge victorious without too much trouble; just be sure to pick up the horse (named Bavieca) on your way out!*

After you emerge victorious from the tournament, you'll be given an army with which you can start this mission. The first thing you'll want to do is move a Villager to the Stone quarry that's to the northwest of your starting position; this Stone deposit is already being mined by King Sancho, but he won't mind if you set up a Mining Camp and work on it as well. If

you hesitate to get this Stone early you won't have a chance to mine any of it later in the game. You'll also want to move El Cid himself into the town above the new mining camp; when you do this the Villagers will give you some of their houses! (See Figure 8-1.)

Figure 8-1   *Moving into King Sancho's town will prove fruitful for The Cid.*

After you've completed your work in King Sancho's town, move your army down the road to the southwest, eventually moving up to the area that's roughly in the middle of the map. As you move along you'll find that a few more soldiers will join your cause. Build up your town center in the map's middle area; here you'll find Gold in abundance, flat lands to farm and build on, and access to the waterways to catch fish.

You should build up your town so that you have the ability to climb the tech tree. The most important structure you'll need to create, however, will be a Siege Workshop. With the Siege Workshop you'll be able to build Mangonels and Battering Rams for punching holes in Alfonso's walls; this is a very important task because Alfonso's forces have Mangonels behind the walls that'll pummel any of your units that get too close.

Bombard the gates with three or four Mangonels (as shown in Figure 8-2), and keep a group of Pikemen nearby to handle the counter-attack that Alfonso will throw at you. After the gates fall, move slowly closer with your Mangonels and Pikemen and target the Guard Towers and Barracks that lie just inside the walls of the city. By doing this you'll take away one of Alfonso's primary defenses for his Castle, which lies just beyond the bridge to the north of the gate you just destroyed.

Figure 8-2 *Taking out Alfonso's gates is a key step to victory.*

To attack the Castle you can either send in a large number of Swordsmen or Pikemen, or you can use several Battering Rams working in unison. Any unit that is not sitting directly against the Castle wall will be destroyed by the Castle's formidable forces; for this reason Mangonels are not the weapon of choice for assaulting the Castle. If you successfully destroy the Guard Towers and Barracks, the only unit that should give you any trouble will be the occasional Monk who tries to convert your units to Alfonso's side.

Tip: *Taking out the enemy's Barracks may not seem necessary, but if you have the siege weapons handy you might as well destroy them so Alfonso can't continue to build new troops that'll slow your assault on the Castle.*

When the Castle falls, Alfonso will offer to go back with you to Sancho's tournament grounds. Lead Alfonso back across the map to the grounds, at which time Alfonso's army will change its status to Ally and the mission will end in victory!

Second Walkthrough: Running the Gauntlet

In this walkthrough you'll try to defeat Alfonso without building any new units. Instead, you'll simply attack him with the units you start with and acquire as you move through the map. Follow the first walkthrough to the point at which El Cid goes to Sancho's northern town and acquires some houses from

Sancho's loyal townsfolk. After this initial stage, move your troops up to the central area of the map where you'll get several Pikemen and Conquistadors.

With your newly combined force you can move up the left side of the map toward Alfonso's left flank. Send two Swordsmen across the river and have each one attack one of the Guard Towers that stand watch over the area; Alfonso won't parry this thrust, leaving you free to destroy the towers. (See Figure 8-3.) It takes a Swordsman a long time to destroy a Guard Tower, but a Tower cannot hit a Swordsman attacking at close range, so the attack is a safe one.

Figure 8-3   *The Swordsmen hack away at the Guard Towers.*

After the Guard Towers have been destroyed, you can build a pair of Watch Towers for yourself near the northwest corner of the map. Put the towers close enough together that they'll be able to cover each other while supplying your troops with a location to fall back to if the enemy attacks become too rabid. Now move forward and attack the Archery Ranges that lie outside the gate. These ranges will continue to produce units if you don't destroy them, so take them out with your Conquistadors (who can fire at a distance, thus staying out of range of enemy Mangonels).

As Alfonso's Archery Ranges take damage, he'll send out Mangonels to attack you. These are a serious threat to your troops, which are a precious resource, so

Tip: *The key to winning the mission in this walkthrough is to use your resources carefully and not rush into head-on battles. In short, you'll be using guerrilla tactics to draw Alfonso's troops into traps that you'll set with your troops.*

you must use Conquistadors to fire at the Archery Range from a distance. Because the Conquistadors are farther away, Alfonso's Mangonels will have to pass through the gate to get close enough to fire. As they pass through the gate, run up a pair of Knights, or even El Cid himself, to take them out quickly.

After the Archery Ranges and several Mangonels have been destroyed, you can send your Conquistadors to work on the gate. This will take a considerable amount of time, but your units will be safe as long as they keep their distance. If any Mangonels or other enemy troops pass through the gates, your Knights can quickly neutralize them. (See Figure 8-4.)

In this manner you can fight, building by building, toward the Castle. As you work your way in you'll be thinning Alfonso's troops and destroying his ability to replace them (because you'll be destroying the Barracks, and so forth. When you reach the Castle your troops will no doubt be weary and

Figure 8-4   *Keep those little warriors out of harm's way.*

Tip: *When assaulting the Castle, you may want to have El Cid patrol the perimeter to take out any enemy Monks or Swordsmen that happen by. El Cid has 450 hit points and will heal over time, so he is the primary choice for such patrols as your other troops attack the Castle.*

their numbers reduced, but if you can get them next to the Castle in time you'll be able to destroy it without taking hits from the castle's formidable arrow defenses. When the Castle is destroyed, you simply escort Alfonso to the tournament grounds and victory will be yours.

Mission Two: The Enemy of My Enemy

Objectives:

- El Cid must survive.
- El Cid must meet with Imam, for he will know how to quell the unrest in Toledo.
- Recover the four Relics from the rebel leaders and return them to Imam.

Hints:

- Since you are unable to construct Trebuchets, garrisoned Battering Rams are probably your best siege weapon.
- Search for guidance from a Moorish holy man living on the lake.
- El Cid may not advance to the Imperial Age.

Scout Reports:

- El Cid (red) starts with a small force that you can use to construct your base. You should do so quickly and scout for resources later.
- El Cid is fighting against the Spanish Rebels (orange) and the Moorish Rebels (green) over the helpless city of Toledo (yellow). There are other Moors nearby, Motamid (cyan) and the Imam (purple), a holy man. Neither seems aggressive against El Cid's forces.
- The Spanish Rebel army is composed of infantry, Knights, and Battering Rams. The Moorish Rebels use Archers, Camels, and Mangonels. Either army may have Monks. Toledo has strong walls, so make sure to bring along siege weapons.

First Walkthrough: Piece by Piece

The city of Toledo has fallen to rebels, and King Alfonso has ordered you, El Cid, to lead his army to capture Toledo—ostensibly to restore order, but we all know that King Alfonso's declaration is a thinly veiled attempt to expand his empire. Your forces begin on a northwestern peninsula that's surrounded entirely by water (consisting mostly of river) that runs roughly through the center of the map.

To successfully build up the forces necessary to capture the Relics, it's a good idea to isolate your "island" so that marauding enemies cannot disrupt your building process with annoying attacks. Secure the area by building a wall in the north central portion of the map where there's a land bridge (as shown in Figure 8-5). This is the primary area where enemy patrols will cross. You should also put gates on the two bridges that allow access to your island, thus making enemy intrusions impossible.

After you have successfully walled off your island, have El Cid hop on the transport ship (which you'll find in the north central area of the map) and ride it to the island at the northernmost area of the map. There Imam will tell you that the only way to quell the rebellion is to obtain the four Relics and return them to him—a tall order indeed. After you've talked with Imam, the location of the Relics will be shown on the map, so you won't have to go searching high and low for them.

Figure 8-5   *An island without enemy troops is a happy island.*

Build up your town and take your technologies to their maximum level. You may need to look outside the island for more resources; there's Stone and Wood in the far east and plenty of Gold in the northeast. Both of these areas are uninhabited and only occasionally have enemy patrols happening by, so it's generally safe to set up lumber or mining camps with only one Knight to guard them.

When you've reached the top of the tech tree you are ready for the assault on the enemy positions. Build six Mangonels, eight Petards, and a bevy of Knights, Conquistadors, and Swordsmen for your fight to reclaim the Relics. Use the bridge in the center of the map as your starting point, and have your troops rally there. First have your Petards take out the Moor Guard Towers that stand near the bridge. Once these have been destroyed, you can line up your Mangonels and take the next two Towers out. (See Figure 8-6).

After the Moorish Guard Towers have been completely eliminated you can turn your force to the south, through the city gates and into Toledo. Remember that the yellow city gates are allies, so you won't have to destroy them to pass through. Run your Knights or Swordsmen in first, because the streets are relatively narrow and you don't want to risk getting your Mangonels destroyed by enemy forces just because of a traffic jam!

Move through the city and destroy the orange buildings that are troop producers (Archery Ranges, Barracks, and Stables). This can be accomplished fairly quickly with your Mangonels while your Knights mop up the enemy units that show up to defend. The first Relic is in a Wooden wall enclosure just

behind the three sets of Stables. There are two more Relics in the Monasteries just to the west—move in and destroy the Monasteries to both retrieve the Relics and destroy the enemy's ability to produce Monks.

You must now send three Monks down to retrieve the Relics and take them to safety on your side of the river. At this point the enemies will be in disarray and will not challenge your Monks as you move to retrieve the

Figure 8-6   *The Mangonels spew tower-eating death.*

Relics. The remaining Relic is guarded by a Castle at the very southern point of the map. This is a Moorish Castle that's accessible only by a bridge guarded by two Guard Towers. The good news is that the resistance is otherwise light, so you need only take out the Guard Towers and then the Wooden wall surrounding the Castle to get access to it. A force of Battering Rams, Mangonels, and Knights work admirably on the Castle, while some Petards will take out the Guard Towers very quickly.

Once all four Relics have been recovered, put the four Monks that are carrying them onto the Transport and ship them up to Imam. When this is completed, victory will be at hand!

Second Walkthrough: The Pincer of Pain

This approach differs from the first walkthrough in two distinct ways: first, you will not wall yourself in entirely, and second, you will build another town on the far east side of the map and then mount a two-pronged attack. Follow the first walkthrough to the point where you meet Imam, but omit building the wall near the land bridge (or build the wall but put a gate on it).

The central and northeast areas of the map are rich in resources, so send over a party of Knights and Villagers to build a town in the far east corner. From this position you can mine Stone and cut Wood, and if you travel a short distance north you'll find a rich Gold deposit (as shown in Figure 8-7). From your two towns you can build up the tech tree quickly while also adding to your armies. The town in the east will, of course, need to have more troops on hand to defend against the odd enemy attack, but otherwise it should flourish.

Figure 8-7   *Looks like Gold in them there hills.*

When you have assembled two armies that include Mangonels, Knights, Petards, and Swordsmen, you can begin your attack. The eastern army can move straight west and move into Toledo through the northern entrance (the same entrance used in the first walkthrough), while the northern army can move across the western bridge and down the left side of the map in a line toward the southernmost point of the map.

This tactic will speed up the battles to obtain the Relics because you'll literally have two armies doing the work of one, but you'll also have to manage both of them at once, which can be a challenge. The eastern army can concentrate on destroying the orange troop-producing units and capturing the three Relics that are in the central area of Toledo, while the northern army can concentrate on bludgeoning its way toward the southern Moorish island and the Relic that's guarded by the Castle. When the Relics have been returned to Imam, the mission will be yours.

Mission Three: The Exile of the Cid

Objectives:

- El Cid must survive.
- Defeat Count Berenguer.
- Destroy Alfonso's Castle so that you may continue on to Zaragoza.
- Join Motamid of the Moors at his Castle in Zaragoza.
- Defend Zaragoza by destroying Count Berenguer's Siege Workshop nearby.

Hints:

- El Cid no longer leads a Spanish army, so become familiar with the Saracen technology tree.
- Know when to fight and when to run away. You might need to destroy walls that block your path, but only if there is no alternative.
- El Cid does not view Alfonso as an enemy so much as misguided. Therefore, you should not destroy anything of Alfonso's unless you are forced to.

Scout Reports:

- El Cid (red) starts alone in exile. Do not fear, for you'll soon find recruits to your cause. You'll have little in the way of an economy until you meet up with an old friend.
- King Alfonso (blue) is your enemy, but he is more of an annoyance than a threat. The real enemy is Count Berenguer of Barcelona (purple). He will send Swordsmen, Knights, Scorpions, and Battering Rams your way.
- Motamid the Moor (green) is a potential ally as are any other Moors you may encounter.

First Walkthrough: Brace, Then Attack

King Alfonso sends El Cid into exile despite his many accomplishments in the name of the King. The Cid rides into the Castillian winter, but he quickly picks up soldiers sympathetic to his plight. Ultimately, El Cid ends up with the Moors, and thus this mission begins. Move north with El Cid to the Stables where you will pick up your horse; then exit the area as soon as possible because Alfonso will open fire at you after a short time.

There's only one direction El Cid can go, so move him along until he runs into some troops that are loyal to him. At that point you can take out the two guards that attack you and move to the narrow mountain pass to the south— there you'll find a small group of Alfonso's troops that you must fight through (as shown in Figure 8-8). After you defeat the small group of enemies, you'll quickly come across four Camels that are willing to join you; they suggest that you join Motamid of the Moors in his Castle. Follow them to the Castle, which will have appeared on your map.

Head south until you come to one of Alfonso's outposts where you will get a message saying that Alfonso has blockaded the escape routes to Motamid's Castle. Destroy the Scout Towers and then continue south where you'll find an encampment that's loyal to your cause; there you'll find one Trebuchet, a Barracks, an Archery Range, and a Siege Workshop to produce the units you'll need to easily take out Alfonso's castle just to the north.

Build one Batter-ing Ram, one Mangonel, and some Swordsmen for the siege. Move north un-til your Trebuchet is in range to attack the gates, and then set it up; as it attacks the gates Alfonso's troops will come out to fight, but your Camels and Swordsmen will make quick work of them. When the Castle falls Alfonso will call a truce and let you go in peace, leaving you to move freely toward Motamid's Castle in the northeast.

Figure 8-8   *You'll have to fight these troops as you pass through the canyon, but there are some Camels waiting to join you on the other side.*

When you reach Motamid's Castle, you'll be charged with the task of taking out Berenguer's assaulting force; if you can do this, you'll be allowed to use the land outside of Motamid's area of influ-ence. Move quickly to the northeast cor-ner of Motamid's domain so that you'll be in a position to attack Berenguer's forces when they attack. As soon as you arrive near Motamid's Castle, Berenguer will at-tack—don't hesitate to send your Camels out to take out his siege weapons while your Knights deal with the melee units. (See Figure 8-9.)

Tip: *Don't get too close to Alfonso's Castle. Remember, Castles have powerful defenses, so it's best to use your Trebuchet to take out an enemy's castle rather than risk taking damage by approaching on foot or horseback.*

Figure 8-9 *Taking out Berenguer's attacking force will mean a nice tribute for your cause.*

When the enemy force (and the nearby Siege Workshop) has been destroyed, Motamid will give you a tribute of Gold, Stone, Wood, and Food. This tribute will be all you need to start up a Town Center and build your armies for an assault to permanently remove Berenguer from the map. Build a Town Center, and then begin to wall in your town so that you can avoid taking surprise attacks from Berenguer.

You'll need to put a short wall between Motamid's wall and a tree line near the middle of the map, and you'll have to run a wall along the length of the northeastern border with Berenguer. This may seem extreme, but this border will allow you to safely spread out to the eastern parts of the map where there's plenty of Gold and lumber to be had. After the wall's built, set up a lumber camp in the extreme east of the map and a mining camp in the area on the edge of the map between the east corner and the south corner.

Ultimately, you'll want to take Berenguer out quickly rather than having to chip away at him slowly. Build up your forces, and build a Castle outside the wall you just constructed to take out any of Berenguer's troops that happen by. (See Figure 8-10.) This Castle will also act as a sentinel that protects your staging area as you get ready to attack Berenguer.

Build a pair of Trebuchets, and then attack Berenguer's gates and walls. As you do this you'll get a response from Berenguer in the form of a flow of troops that your Castle will take care of in a jiffy. Once you've punched two holes in his walls, it's time to go after Berenguer. A great way to take out his Castle is to attack him with a group of six Petards while a group of Elite Mamelukes works

as a diversion. The Petards will destroy the Castle, and the Mamelukes can be moved back and healed by Monks once the job is done.

Use your over-powering resource base to sweep into Berenguer's camp and destroy all of his buildings. The Trebuchet is your best weapon for this, but you must protect it with ground troops and be ready to repair it with Villagers. Once Berenguer has been sufficiently beaten down, he'll surrender to you and victory will be yours.

Figure 8-10 *Building a Castle outside your town walls will prevent any attacks from Berenguer while providing a safe staging area for your attacks.*

Second Walkthrough: The Back Door

This walkthrough follows the same path as the first walkthrough from the time El Cid is exiled until he (and his troops) are able to destroy Berenguer's forces outside Motamid's city. However, once you have received the tribute and are ready to build your town, you take a slightly different approach to building your army for the attack on Berenguer.

Instead of mounting your army strictly in the north of the map for a frontal assault, you use the existing camp in the southern portion of the map to produce a second army. This camp has some great advantages: the Archery Range has Hand Cannoneers, and the Siege Workshop has Bombard Cannons and also allows you to upgrade to Siege Rams and Siege Onagers. These are all items that you otherwise would not be able to produce!

Tip: *The Hand Cannoneers are very useful for defending the Bombard Cannons because they have a long range and are very powerful against enemy units of all kinds. Always keep them close to your Bombard Cannons or Onagers.*

Build a group of six Bombard Cannons and eight Hand Cannoneers, and then move them up to the land bridge that lies to the northwest of Motamid's city walls. This land bridge has gates on either end, one that belongs to Alfonso (which you can cross through) and one that belongs to Berenguer (which you'll have to destroy). Move your troops in the north up to attack Berenguer at exactly the same time your Bombard Cannons unload on the land-bridge gates. After the gates fall, take out the Guard Tower and the Castle, and then keep moving.

This pincer attack will give Berenguer's forces nowhere to run because you'll be hitting him simultaneously on his two walled flanks. The key is to use your Bombard Cannons to move quickly into Berenguer's town and destroy the unit-producing structures such as the Archery Range and the Barracks. (See Figure 8-11.) With your northern army doing the same, you'll have an easy time bringing Count Berenguer to his knees!

Figure 8-11   *Use your Bombard Cannons to quickly wipe out Berenguer's buildings.*

Mission Four: Black Guards

Objectives:

- El Cid must survive.
- Bring El Cid to the Black Guard Mosque.
- King Alfonso must survive.
- Destroy the six Black Guard Docks.
- Destroy the Black Guard Transports.

Hints:

- Save King Alfonso as quickly as possible.
- The sea can be an important battlefield and a good source of Food. Including a navy in your strategy may prove useful.

Scout Reports:

- El Cid's forces (red) are allied with those of King Alfonso (blue).
- There are three enemies, the Black Guard Army (cyan), the Black Guard Navy (yellow), and Yusuf's Elite Guard (green). The two land armies field mostly Camel and siege units. The navy trains Galleys and Spearmen.
- All three of your enemies have walled cities with many towers, so try using Trebuchets and garrisoned Battering Rams against them. Eventually, you may need to build a navy as well. You can construct your Docks within the city of a vanquished enemy or in no-man's-land between the cities.

First Walkthrough: In Between

King Alfonso is so upset by seeing El Cid's Moorish and Christian armies grow in power and prestige that he declares war on the Moors. El Cid will not wage war on Alfonso, and when the Moors look for help from the Berbers they get help that will eventually force Alfonso to look to El Cid for help. This mission begins with Alfonso in trouble, and El Cid's forces are poised to rescue him.

Group your units together, and follow Alfonso's Knight to the battle where King Alfonso awaits. Don't waste any time—when you get to Alfonso, immediately get him and your units to his town in the far west corner of the map. When you arrive you can begin to build your resources for the coming battles. Be sure to exploit the fish stocks in the lake by the town; even though it's land-locked, there's enough Food there to make it worthwhile to build a Dock.

There are Gold and Wood resources nearby, directly to the south of the camp, so send several Villagers down to start mining and chopping right away. There is also a Black Guard Mosque that, when El Cid approaches, will offer to be converted to your cause (as shown in Figure 8-12). To do this you'll need to bring down a Monk who has the ability to convert buildings; when you successfully convert the building you'll be able to learn two skills from the Mosque!

Build up your forces to the point where most of the technology tree has been attained (at least for the Blacksmith and Monastery), and then gather up a large force of units for a single surgical attack on the one area that's the least defended on the entire coastline. The two enemies have towns that are side by side, but there's a narrow area that's relatively undefended with a beach where you can build a Dock. You must covet and secure this area.

Move your army down this narrow band of real estate and push toward the beach where you can

Figure 8-12   *When El Cid approaches this Mosque, they'll offer to be converted for your uses.*

set up a Dock. You can often slip a Villager or two out to the beach to build a Dock while your other troops occupy the enemy. As soon as the Dock is built you'll need to build as many Galleons as you can afford. As the Galleons become damaged, you can repair them with Villagers if you have some near the Dock area.

> **Tip:** *When you push toward the beach, be aware that if you attack one of the enemy's structures you'll incite them to send units over to attack you, so sometimes it's better to lay low.*

Move your ships through the waters, and take out all enemy ships while you pound away on the six Black Guard Docks (as shown in Figure 8-13). Keep harvesting all the resources you can so that you can build more ships—the more you build, the better your chances of success. Once the Docks have been destroyed, it's all over!

Figure 8-13 *Taking out the six heavily fortified Black Guard Docks will ensure victory.*

Second Walkthrough: The Bludgeon

As with the last walkthrough, group your units together and follow Alfonso's Knight to the battle where King Alfonso awaits. Don't waste any time—when you get to Alfonso, immediately get him and your units to his town in the far west corner of the map. When you arrive you can begin to build your resources for the coming battles. And be sure to exploit the fish stocks in the lake by the town.

This is a straight-up slugfest. You must conquer one of the two enemies (Black Guard or Yusuf) in order to secure the coastline. This method is considerably more difficult and will require you to devote much more time to resource gathering. However, it will supply more security from attacks once you get your Dock established.

> **Tip:** *When attacking Yusuf go straight for the Stables and Barracks, because as long as they exist Yusuf will produce large numbers of units to combat your offensive, which will most certainly wear you down.*

Remember that there are Gold and Wood resources nearby (directly to the south of the camp) as well as large Wood and Stone (and even Food) deposits in the north. Again, there is also a Black Guard Mosque that, when El Cid approaches, will offer to be converted to your cause. To do this you'll need to bring down a Monk who has the ability to convert buildings; when you successfully convert the building you'll be able to learn two skills from the Mosque.

The best way to win this mission is to bludgeon the weaker of your enemies (in this case Yusuf) into oblivion by overpowering his structures with siege weapons and outnumbering his ground troops with your own troops. By taking out Yusuf, you can gain control over the entire eastern portion of the map, which includes sizable Gold and Wood deposits.

Once Yusuf's town is under your control, you can sit back and build up your naval technology (and build a pair of Docks to launch your armada). When the Transports and the Black Guard Docks have been destroyed, victory will be at hand. This method (wiping out Yusuf first), takes considerably longer and requires perfect tactics to ensure that you don't use up your resources.

Mission Five: King of Valencia

Objectives:

- El Cid must survive.
- El Cid must once again find a new city in which to live.
- El Cid must flee and establish a new base.
- Defend Valencia from Berenguer until the Wonder is completed.

Hints:

- El Cid no longer serves the Moors. Your technology tree is Spanish once again.
- Look for soldiers and Villagers who will join The Cid. You'll need an army to take Valencia.
- Know when to fight and when to run away.
- Count Berenguer's army is mighty, but he does not own a navy. Therefore, you can get plenty of Food from the Mediterranean, but fielding your own navy is not necessary.
- Berenguer's mountain fortress is virtually impenetrable. Although you can slow him down by a direct assault, that is not the path to victory.

Scout Reports:

- El Cid (red) is alone again, and this time Motamid cannot come to his assistance.
- There are several towns in southern Spain that might be willing to become allies—Denia (green), Lerida (orange), and Valencia (yellow). None of these towns can field a large military.
- El Cid's enemy is once again Count Berenguer (purple). Berenguer has a well-fortified city in the north that will prove very difficult to siege. Therefore, other avenues to victory are a better option. Berenguer relies on combined arms of Archers, Infantry, and Knights along with a plethora of siege weapons. Construct your defenses well!

First Walkthrough: Hunker Down

The Cid, in exile again, wanders Castille. Many mercenaries and knights know of the tales of The Cid and are eager to follow him. The Cid has enough of an army that he decides to invade Valencia before King Alfonso invades first. Unfortunately, Count Berenguer chooses the same time to strike back at The Cid, making the situation far more complicated.

As this mission begins you will be alone: The Cid on horseback. Move toward the east and the land bridge, and you'll come across some of Berenguer's men who have aims to take you out. Fortunately, you come across the town of Denia where the soldiers and townsfolk embrace you. After Berenguer's troops have been deposed, you must take all of the troops in Denia and run across the bridge to the south. If you do not do this, they will all be destroyed by a

Tip: *If you work quickly, you can have the Mosque in Denia create a Monk that you can get across the bridge before it's destroyed. All of the buildings (except houses) will be destroyed in Denia.*

massive attack by Berenguer. Don't forget to grab the four Villagers near the Mill as well, because you can use them once you get to Valencia.

Once you reach the southern area of the map, you'll come across the town of Lerida, occupied by Saracens. These people will grant you three Camels and two Villagers if El Cid walks through the streets. After you've picked up your extra troops, move up to Valencia where you'll be welcomed with open arms. (See Figure 8-14.) Move your troops inside the safety of Valencia's walls, but be sure to head just east of Valencia where a Monastery and two Monks will join your cause and give you 650 Wood!

Once in Valencia, send two of your Villagers to the area just south of the Monastery where there's both Stone and Wood to be had. Have them build a Lumber Camp and a Mining Camp and start gathering; these Villagers will likely work throughout this mission without being attacked by Berenguer's troops. Inside Valencia you can set the Dock to build several Fishing Ships and have Villagers mine Stone and Gold and harvest Sheep, keeping your resources replenished as time goes on.

Figure 8-14   *Valencia is where you'll be burrowing in.*

Now create a pair of Villagers to build extra Watch Towers inside the compound around the Wonder that's being built. Putting in four extra towers is a good idea, and six would be even better! Once the towers are in place, you'll need to build an inner wall to give the Wonder area a double-layered wall that will hold up under Berenguer's siege weaponry. Once this is done, you'll need to

keep a pair of Villagers nearby to work on spot repairs (as shown in Figure 8-15). You want to wall up the gates to Valencia, because if you don't your troops will slip in and out and occasionally let the enemy in. Once walled in, your troops will stay behind the walls and shoot at the enemies rather than try to chase them.

You'll now want to turn your attention to putting at least one of your Monks near the Wonder so that they can heal any

Figure 8-15 *After you've created an inside wall and Watch Towers for extra protection, keep a couple of Villagers around to do spot repairs.*

units in this area that take damage from enemy siege weapons. Build some Archers that you can place around the Wonder to give you more ranged attack ability for the stray enemy units that will attempt to circle the encampment. It's also a good idea to research the Thumb Ring in the Archery Range, so that your Archers are more accurate.

The Berenguer troops will likely attack in two or three waves, each time throwing some serious firepower at your walls. Keep Villagers busy repairing, and attempt to take the enemy units out as best you can. You should keep units such as Knights and Camels on the outside of the walled-in encampment so that they can act as a "Strike Team" that can be brought in to wreak havoc on the enemy siege weapons when they get set up to attack you. Just keep your defense up and you'll be able to prevent Berenguer from destroying the Wonder, and you'll taste victory yet again.

Second Walkthrough: Offense as Defense

The beginning of this walkthrough is the same as the last one: move toward the east and the land bridge, and you'll come across some of Berenguer's men

AGE

of

EMPIRES II

Tip: *If you're feeling extra frisky, you can even build a Castle outside the Wonder's walls and have that extra measure of protection from the Count's attacks. A Castle, however, can lead to Berenguer giving you more attention than he otherwise would, so weigh that when you're making your decision.*

who have aims to take you out. Fortunately, you come across the town of Denia where the soldiers and townsfolk embrace you. After Berenguer's troops have been destroyed, you must take all of the troops in Denia and run across the bridge to the south to prevent them from being killed by Berenguer's coming attack.

When you get to Lerida, have El Cid ride through the town and pick up the Camels that the people of Lerida offer you. You'll also want to grab the Villagers that are offered up and move them to the area south of the Monastery where they can mine Stone and cut Wood. In Valencia, immediately set your Villagers to gathering Wood, Gold, and Food; set your Dock to produce some Fishing Ships to gather Food in the sea to the east as well.

As soon as the resources come in (you'll get 650 Wood from the Monastery), have your Archery, Stables, and Castle produce fighting units. These units will be used to mount an offensive attack that will surprise Berenguer and delay his siege on your Wonder long enough for you to emerge victorious.

Keep your Knights outside your front gate and move out and aggressively attack anything that comes near your position. The only caveat to this aggressive posture is that you need to keep an eye out for the enemy Bombard Towers, which are very powerful and should generally be avoided. (See Figure 8-16.) By constantly filing new troops to the area outside the Wonder enclosure you'll be

Figure 8-16   *By taking the battle to the enemy you can throw his calculated siege attack off balance.*

able to ensure victory on your own terms rather than having to sit back and wait to be attacked.

Mission Six: Reconquista

Objectives:

- Defeat the three armies of Yusuf so that Valencia will remain free.
- The body of The Cid (near the Castle) must come to no harm, lest the people of Valencia realize they have lost their leader.

Hints:

- You will need to expand from the Valencian fortress in order to procure more resources.
- Concentrate on fighting in Spain at first. Later you can attempt to sail across to Yusuf's base in Africa.
- Spanish Cannon Galleons are powerful. You should use them when attacking Yusuf in Africa.

Scout Reports:

- El Cid (red) has all the buildings he needs in Valencia to quickly field an army.
- There are three enemies: The Black Guard Army (cyan), Black Guard Navy (yellow), and Yusuf's Elite Forces (green).
- The Black Guard Army is north of Valencia and the most immediate threat, but it can be dispatched by a series of quick raids. The Black Guard Army is composed mostly of Camels and Cavalry Archers.
- The Black Guard Navy is west of Valencia but can be reached by land. The Navy is better defended than the Army but can still be attacked early. In addition to the cavalry, the Black Guard Navy has some Monks.
- Yusuf is the most dangerous enemy. His ships may attack Valencia early on, and his fortress in Africa is dangerous. Yusuf trains Camels, Cavalry Archers, and Monks that he will attempt to transport across in addition to the Fire Ships and Cannon Galleons.

First Walkthrough: The Ultimate Defense

The Cid, after all of his incredible accomplishments, has been killed by a stray arrow during a clandestine raid to steal Horses and Gold from the Berbers. His men do not know he is dead, and he has been strapped to his horse to act as a macabre figurehead that will lead his men in battle to defend Valencia from Yusuf and the Berber hoards.

Unfortunately The Cid will not be of help to you, even though he's propped up on his Horse in front of the Castle. However, there are plenty of structures and resources available to make your job possible. The first thing you need to do is get your Villagers all doing something useful while your buildings upgrade whatever they can. Getting the technology tree to the top in this mission is essential for victory.

Take your existing army and move quickly to take out the Black Guard Army that lies directly to your west. This encampment will fall relatively easily, and you can eliminate them as a threat within a few minutes; this is an important step because the fewer enemies you're facing, the better. Destroying this area will free up plenty of space and resources for you to harvest, so it's important that you do it.

The next thing you should do is build a wall to wall off the pesky Black Guard Navy Guard in the south (as shown in Figure 8-17). This is a short-term measure that'll allow you to finish off the Black Guard Army camp in the north and get your resources on track.

Move north now, and finish off the Black Guard Army in the northern area of your land mass. This will also be a relatively easy kill and will free up resources so that you can comfortably expand your empire without fear of immediate attack. At this point you may want to either wall up the entire coast from Valencia to the north edge of the map, or put Guard Towers up to keep an eye on Yusuf who'll be landing transports full of soldiers from time to time.

Ideally, you'll want to wall yourself in so that you can concentrate on managing resources while building your armies to take out the Black Guard Navy in the South. When you have an assault team of siege weapons, Knights, Swordsmen, Monks, and whatever else you can build, move them down to the south and systematically chip away at the enemy structures until you've overwhelmed them. Taking a group of eight Petards to

Tip: *Deal with your enemies in this mission one at a time to increase your chances of victory. This mission is particularly difficult, so you'll want to stack the odds in your favor any way you can.*

the Castle in a kami-kaze effort will usually take the Castle down in a few seconds.

Once the Black Guard Navy base has fallen (and it will take a while to do this), you can start building Docks along the beach in anticipation of your attack on Yusuf in Africa. Build up your fleet by build-ing Galleons and Fire Ships, but keep them close to the Docks—don't let them venture out.

Once you have a set of transports loaded with siege weapons, Knights, and Conquistadors, send the Galleons and Fire Ships to the enemy beach on the southeast tip of Yusuf's area. This is the least defended area and an excellent place to land your troops and establish a foothold for your conquest of Yusuf. (See Figure 8-18.)

Once you have a foothold in this area, build a Castle and

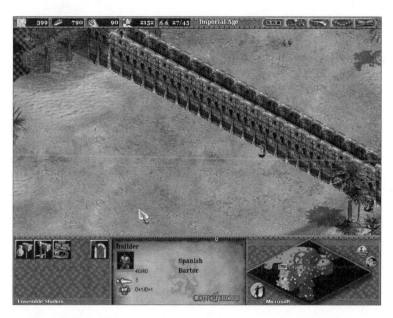

Figure 8-17   *Build a wall to provide some defense from the Black Guard Navy in the south.*

Figure 8-18   *This area in the south of Yusuf's African coast is the place to land your troops.*

construct some buildings that supply your favorite units. Attack Yusuf bit by bit while also ferrying over units from your mainland. When Yusuf falls, you'll have completed the campaign. Congratulations!

Second Walkthrough: Kamikaze Attack

As with the last mission, The Cid will not be of help to you, even though he's propped up on his Horse in front of the Castle. However, there are plenty of structures and resources available to make your job possible. The first thing you need to do is get your Villagers all doing something useful while your buildings upgrade whatever they can.

For this walkthrough, you'll attempt something very difficult indeed. You will first strike out to the west and take the central Black Guard Army camp, wall yourself off from the Black Guard Army in the north and the Black Guard Navy in the south, and then concentrate exclusively on building up a navy to attack Yusuf.

This technique is very difficult because Yusuf's navy starts off very strong—you'll have to spend your resources improving your navy so that you can launch an all-out assault on Yusuf's African base. Build Galleons and Fire Ships and take out Yusuf's Docks to destroy his ability to combat your navy, and then begin to land troops on his shores, building Castles whenever possible to establish footholds. After Yusuf falls, the resources on the African side of the map will give you everything you need to eliminate the Black Guard Navy in the south.

Chapter Nine

The Campaigns of the Conquerors

No doubt, the campaigns are quite a bit of fun, but the fun's not over when El Cid fights his final battle. Ensemble Studios has compiled a set of semihistorical battles from the annals of history. As before, we supply two walkthroughs for each battle for your gaming enjoyment. Keep your eyes glued to these pages. It's all strategy, all the time.

Agincourt

Objectives:

- King Henry must survive.
- Acquire a Transport Ship to send King Henry V back home to England.
- Destroy the Blacksmith in Amiens to recover armor and weapons. (Optional)
- Destroy the University in Voyeni to recover and learn from the great texts stored there. (Optional)

Hints:

- Because you're in enemy lands, cut off from supplies, you won't be able to establish a town or train new units. You must survive with your initial army.
- Because you lack resources, converting enemy Villagers will serve only to let you convert siege weapons.

AGE
of
EMPIRES II

Scout Reports:

- The English (red) must navigate or conquer several French towns before they can return home. Harfleur (purple) is in the southwest, Amiens (cyan) is atop a cliff plateau in the south, Voyeni (green) is in the center of the area, Frevent (yellow) is to the southeast, and the French Knights (blue) roam the north.
- England lies to the northwest, across the English Channel. You'll need Transports to reach it.
- Bridges are out or heavily fortified down most of the length of the River Somme. There might be, however, an undefended crossing further southeast.

First Walkthrough: Run for Your Life

Let's get something straight right from the beginning: you don't have to defeat anybody to win this scenario. To win, you must merely load King Henry V on the transport docked southeast of the Briton's castle, sail him to the castle, and unload. It doesn't matter if you lose every other Briton in the game. Accordingly, this first walkthrough will focus on accomplishing the victory conditions with minimal fighting. The second walkthrough will stress fighting your way to victory.

Pause the game as soon as it starts. Group like units (for example, Elite Longbowmen, Two-Handed Swordsman, and so on). Group Henry V with the Knights. Retreat all your units a ways north, and order them to Stand Ground. Leave your Monks just behind the Swordsmen (as shown in Figure 9-1).

Harfleur sorties Cavalry against your minions. Convert one, and kill the rest. Move north, and take the first right. This leads to Voyeni's first gate. Take down the gate with your Battering Rams. Use the Longbowman to waste anyone who interferes. Once inside the Voyeni base, destroy the Archery Range and Blacksmith. Continue south, and raze the University. Doing so gives you Greek Fire, which increases the Elite Longbowmen's attack by one.

Ignore the Voyeni castle, and cross the bridge. Follow the road north to the mud. Lasso all your footsoldiers, put them in a box formation, and send them to the east side of the mud. Select all the mounted units—including Henry V—and

Tip: *Use your Monks to convert as many mounted units as possible. You'll soon need them.*

position them on the west side of the mud. The French Knights are north of the mud. Engage them with the Elite Longbowmen that are in the box of footsoldiers on the east side of the mud. The French will charge the footsoldiers. When the French charge, run Henry V north through the Knight's camp. Take a left (that is, move southwest) just past the second set of twin towers. You might lose a Knight to the twin towers, but fear not: the end is near.

Follow the road through another set of towers, and then skirt the stockade encampment. Keep the fence to your right and the water to your left, and head north. By now, you'll have a few pursuers. It's just like the movies—a heroic king narrowly escaping death! Board the waiting transport (as shown in Figure 9-2), sail to England, and you win. No fuss, no muss.

Figure 9-1   *This is a solid beginning.*

Figure 9-2   *This King boards his craft.*

Second Walkthrough: The Big Battles

Figure 9-3   *The Voyeni castle under attack.*

Begin as you did in the first walkthrough. Once, however, you've destroyed the University in Voyeni, take out the Voyeni castle (as shown in Figure 9-3). Otherwise, it'll damage your troops as you stream south to attack Amiens.

March southwest once the Voyeni castle has been rubbled. You'll soon stumble into Amien's gates. Take out the Guard Towers with your Elite Longbowmen and the gates with your Battering Rams. Follow the road straight to the Blacksmith. Destroy the building and your Two-Handed Swordsmen are rewarded with two more attack points and all concerned are rewarded with better armor.

> **Tip:** *You might want to place your Monks beside the Amiens' Archery Range or Barracks. Convert any newly produced Amiens units for the upcoming battle with the French Knights.*

Now head toward the mud flats in front of the French Knights. This is the road to Agincourt and your salvation. Convert anyone that you meet along the way. Place your Swordsmen and Longbowmen in one group, place them in a line formation, and station them about halfway up the road to the mudflats. Anchor the Monks behind them to heal the formation. Herd any Villagers in front for cannon fodder. Run your Knights (and Henry V) to the flats.

Show the English Knights to the left side of the French Knights, and then retreat to your Swordsmen and Longbowmen. Some Frenchmen will follow.

Slay them, rinse, and repeat. It usually takes two trips to kill them all. Head north. Capture the Trebuchet next to the Barracks by first destroying the walls of its compound and then moving next to the Trebuchet. Destroy the Castle Amiens (as shown in Figure 9-4) and its surrounding towers by using the Trebuchet.

Move west down the road. Again, French Knights will attack. Destroy them with a combination of footsoldiers and your

Figure 9-4   *The trebuchet works on the Castle Amiens.*

own Knights. Use the Trebuchet to take out the Guard Towers. Turn Henry north to the small bay cited in the first walkthrough, board the Transport, and sail to England—victory is yours.

Hastings

Objectives:

- William the Conqueror must survive.
- Conquer England by destroying the Castle of Harold the Saxon.

Hints:

- While you prepare your army to invade England, be watchful of Saxon attacks into Normandy.
- The Isle of Wight, along England's southern shore, is a safe staging ground for your invasion.

AGE *of* EMPIRES II

Scout Reports:

- The Normans (blue) have a large town established in France. Their lands should be free of enemy marauders, but Harold's Raiders (yellow) could attack at any moment.
- The Saxon Navy (red) will try to repel any Norman Transports or Warships that threaten Harold's Army (orange). You can try to defeat the Saxon Navy's shipyards to the north and south before laying siege to Harold the Saxon's Castle near London.
- The Vikings under Harald Hardraade (cyan) are a wildcard. They're at war with Harold the Saxon, but can they be trusted?

First Walkthrough: Befriending Berserkers

Tip: *There are Forage Bushes west of your starting point. Build a Mill near them (as shown in Figure 9-5) to add to your Food production.*

Churn out five Villages, and put them and your initial five to work chopping lumber, harvesting Food, and mining Gold. Construct a Stable, and crank out a handful of Knights. Use these Knights and your original allotment of Cavalry (including William) to bait and destroy the small detachment of Harold's Raiders that begin north of your position.

Grab a Villager and continue north. Build a Dock at the northern end of the peninsula. Construct two War Galleys and five Transports. Cross to Harald Hardraade's camp. This releases his Elite Berserkers, a slew of Longboats, and Harald's grateful tribute.

Figure 9-5   *The Villagers forage for Food.*

Load a Villager and the Berserkers on the Transports, escort them with your Galleys and Harald's fleet, and head west by southwest. With luck, you'll make landfall on a beach near a trail leading west (as shown in Figure 9-6).

Build a Watchtower in the pass, and place the Berserkers in front of it. When the tower is done, construct a Stables and crank out the Cavalry—that's what the Franks are good at.

Figure 9-6   *The Norman/Viking beachhead.*

Once the Berserkers have beaten off the initial Saxon assault, it's time to send them north in search of Gold. You'll find it near the north tip of the land. Destroy the Watchtower, build a Mining Camp, and start mining. You might want to protect the miners with a pair of Berserkers. Meanwhile, send your fleet west along this north coast. You'll find some Saxon Docks—take them out.

> **Note:** *Don't forget to continue to research, boost your economy, and upgrade your civilization. By now you should be in the Imperial Age and have a large fleet—that is, 10 to 12 warships.*

Now send the Berserkers and Knights south along the path that leads from your initial landing. You'll find a pile of Rocks to mine. Build a Siege Workshop here, and spend the time and money to research the Onager upgrade.

Meanwhile, add a few Galleons to your navy, lasso every ship that you own, and head south from the Docks that you initially built. You'll find the final Saxon naval base on a peninsula in the middle of the map. Take it down, and you won't have to worry about the Saxon Navy again.

Back to the Rock pile and our Berserkers and Knights. Follow the path southwest to a Saxon outpost. Swarm the outpost. Bring up your Onagers and a couple of Rams for good measure. Continue southwest, break through Harold's gates, take down his castle, and you win.

Second Walkthrough: Another Solution

The first walkthrough is the prime solution to this mission and how the mission was designed to be played. Nevertheless, there are other alternatives. Here's one. Begin as you did in the first mission. Construct a Dock, and load the Berserkers (as shown in Figure 9-7).

Take the Viking Longboats and your own warships and Transports and set sail to the northern Saxon Navy Docks. Land the Berserkers, and order them to assist your navy's destruction of the Docks. Once the Docks are destroyed, order your navy to sail to a position north (and out of the sight) of the second set of Saxon Docks (on the east coast of England). Don't try to destroy the Docks; there's no need to sick your resources into a massive navy.

Figure 9-7 *The Berserkers have a different objective in this walkthrough.*

This blocking force will suffice to intercept any Saxon ships that attempt to interfere with your plans.

Send whatever Cavalry you have to the Berserker landing sight in the north. Include a Villager. While the Cavalry's in transit, march your Berserkers south to the bridge. Bait and eliminate the waiting Saxons. Pause to heal, and rendezvous with the Cavalry. Have the Villager that you sent over with the Cavalry build a Siege Workshop just north of the bridge. Crank out a couple of Rams and Onagers, and cross the bridge. Sick the siege weapons on the Saxon towers and the northern gate to their city.

Once the gate collapses (as shown in Figure 9-8), throw everyone and everything at the Castle. Soon it will fall, and victory will be yours.

Figure 9-8 *With the gate destroyed, the way lays open to the Castle.*

Kyoto

Objectives:

- Your Lord, Nobunaga, is trapped in Kyoto. You must rescue him to restore his honor.
- Destroy all three of Kyoto's Castles to punish Kyoto for the death of Lord Nobunaga.
- Establish a base from which to attack Kyoto.

AGE *of* EMPIRES II

Hints:

- Some of your Samurai are in Kyoto with Lord Nobunaga. They won't be able to escape on their own, but they can attempt to protect Nobunaga.
- Defeat the garrison at Osaka, and establish your own town in its place. Do not wantonly destroy buildings, or you'll have to rebuild much once you capture Osaka.
- Although a direct assault on Kyoto can be successful, sneak attacks might yield fewer casualties.
- Rebel Monks in Kyoto are actively searching for Relics. Do not allow them such a victory.

Scout Reports:

- Hideyoshi's forces (cyan) begin onboard Lord Nobunaga's ships. After you invade Osaka, you'll need to quickly neutralize resistance and establish a base.
- There are three enemies in this region: Osaka (red) has walls and Castles but has a small standing army. Hyogo (blue) is a relatively small village. An early strike can eliminate this threat, but Hyogo will eventually attack with infantry, Archers, and Samurai if allowed to build unchecked. Kyoto (green) is the most dangerous enemy; the city is well defended, and many Spearmen, Samurai, and Knights defend the Castles. Kyoto might also build a navy if given the opportunity.

First Walkthrough: Bashing Down the Walls

Make no mistake: Nobunaga will die. But don't stress—his death is in the scenario design. Instead, take your initial landing force and rush through the hole in the wall blown by your saboteurs. Fight what meager resistance is thrown at you, and send a Knight to the Town Center. This captures the Town Center and kills the rest of the Villagers.

Crank out eight Villagers of your own. Order them to mine Gold, cut Lumber, and build a Dock and an Archery near your initial landing site. Next,

construct four Fishing Boats and a Transport. Load the Bombard Cannons on the Transport. Send the loaded Transport and the rest of your Knights and Arablests west to the swamplike crossing or causeway that leads to the Hyogo's camp (as shown in Figure 9-9).

Guard the Bombard Cannons with the Arablests and Knights. Those cannons are too valuable

Figure 9-9 *Across this passage is the way to victory.*

to lose. These initial units will be plenty to take down Hyogo. Once Hyogo is destroyed, regroup your fighters on the causeway. Now buff up your economy. A Stone quarry lies west of the Osaka Monastery. Mine the rock, and build both a Castle and a University near the Hyogo causeway. Research Chemistry at the University, Elite Samurai at the Castle, and then Elite Cannon Galley at the Dock. Assemble a fleet/army consisting of three Elite Cannon Galleons, three Fire Ships, all the Bombard Cannons, and any other footsoldiers that you can muster, including a handful of Elite Samurai.

Follow the sea northeast until you spot the walls of Kyoto's city. Use the Elite Cannon Galleons to knock out the Castle closest to the bridge, all the Guard Towers that pose a threat, and the gates to the city. Land your troops, and move northeast into the city. Another Castle awaits your attention. Protect your Bombard Cannons with your footsoldiers while the cannons destroy this second Castle. Load the survivors onto the Transports.

Note: *Loading the survivors is not necessary to win. But it makes you feel like a better person when you save their little lives.*

Figure 9-10 *The Elite Cannon Galleons' range keeps them safe from the Castle's arrows.*

Figure 9-11 *These Petards will play an important part in your upcoming victory.*

Move the fleet southeast until you spot the final Castle. Because of their superior range, the Elite Cannon Galleons can bombard it (as shown in Figure 9-10) without fear of reprise. Take it down, and the mission will end.

Second Walkthrough: The Subtle Approach

The second walkthrough is similar to the first but requires a bit less brawn and, if not more brains, at least a bit more subtlety. Begin as before. Capture the town center, kick-start the economy, and then destroy Hyogo.

Build a Castle and Stable. Have the Stable churn out 10 Light Cavalry and a handful of Knights. Order the Castle to train 10–15 Petards (as partially shown in Figure 9-11), and construct two Trebuchets.

Load three Petards and the Cavalry/Knights on Transports, and sail them to the north. You'll find a shore and more Kyoto walls and a gate. Use three Petards to blast through the gate. Once through, unleash your mounted troops in the interior of the city. Don't, however, ask them to destroy. Order them to attack nothing, and set a patrol route that leads them throughout the city. This will draw most of the city's defenders (which are all slower footsoldiers) into a wild goose chase in a vain attempt to destroy the Cavalry. While most of the defenders are so occupied, land the Bombard Cannons as before (as shown in Figure 9-12).

Destroy the gate and nearby Castle. Land the Trebuchets and any available footsoldiers, and take out the far Castle. Now move all your units towards the southern Castle. Keep the Petards in the Transports. Attack the southern Castle from the north. When it and its guarding troops respond, sneak the Petards into the bay, run them up to the Castle, and destroy it.

Figure 9-12 *The Cannons make landfall.*

Lepanto

Objectives:

- Complete and then defend your Wonder for 200 years.
- Tribute 800 Gold to the Greeks. (Optional)

Hints:

- Do not use all of your Villagers to construct a Wonder. You'll need some to gather resources and to repair walls, towers, and ships.
- It's very difficult to go on the offensive against the Turkish fleet.
- Greek isles hold additional resources, if you can defend them.

Scout Reports:

- Don Juan's Spanish and Italian fleet (red) has abandoned the sea to build a Wonder on the beach.
- They must defend it from the Ottoman empire. The Turks (purple) use a variety of different ships, including Cannon Galleons, and will attempt to transport Janissaries and Bombard Cannons across the sea. However, quick counterattacks against the Turks might slow their progress.
- The Greek villages (green) are caught in the middle of the battle but might join you if presented with the right opportunity.

First Walkthrough: By the Book

This isn't a particularly tough mission. As the game suggests, do not order all your Villagers to build the Wonder. Place three on the Wonder, and evenly divide the remainder among Food collection, chopping Wood, and mining the Gold that waits outside your west gate (as shown in Figure 9-13).

Research Dry Dock at your Dock. The extra speed will help your ships intercept the incoming Turkish Transports. Group like ships (that is, make one group of Cannon Galleons, another of Fire Ships, and so on). Have another Dock build five more Fast Fire ships. The Turks will send an armada your way. Attack and eliminate it. Now station your Fire Ships in a line extending south of the island that lies just east of your University. Sprinkle in some War Galleys, place the Cannon Galleys closer to shore, and set the entire flotilla to a Defensive Stance. Build 10 Demolition ships, and sprinkle them along your coast. Group the Onagers, and position them near the Wonder.

Tip: *Form a group of 10–15 Conquistadors, and use them as a fire brigade. Send them wherever a Turkish Transport lands to wipe out the Onager-thinned ranks.*

In a few minutes, a pair of Turkish Transports will try to break through your line of ships. If you've positioned everything correctly, they'll never make it. Soon, the Greeks will offer a treaty. Accept it by paying the 800 Gold tribute. Train four Villagers, load them on a

Transport, and transport them to the just-revealed Greek island. Build a mining camp, and mine Stone and Gold.

Continue to crank out Heavy Demolition ships, and liberally seed your coast with them. Leftover money should go toward Onagers, Conquistadors, and Two-Handed Swordsmen. Make no mistake, the Turks will land Transports. When they do, thin the ranks of the invaders with the Onagers.

The final victory, shown in Figure 9-14, is close at hand. Detail Villagers to repair damaged Guard and Bombard Towers. Given the Stone you've collected, you might even be able to construct more Guard Towers—garrison them with Archers or Hand Cannoneers—or research and erect Bombard Towers. Keep killing Turks, and their attack will slack, usually when you have about 75 guarding years remaining on the Wonder.

Figure 9-13   *The Villagers happily dig for Gold.*

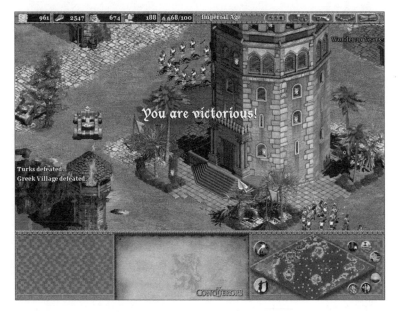

Figure 9-14   *A well-earned victory.*

AGE *of* EMPIRES II

Second Walkthrough: Breakin' All the Rules

Begin as in the first walkthrough, and continue until you've defeated the first probing attack by the Turkish armada. Research Cannon Galleon at the Dock.

Figure 9-15   *The sandy beaches of Turkey are a welcome sight.*

You'll need a powerful navy to win this walkthrough. As soon as the resources are available, research Elite Cannon Galleon and churn out 10 more Heavy Demolition ships.

Take your fleet southeast. You'll find the Turkish coastline (as shown in Figure 9-15). Follow the coastline northeast to the harbor in which the Turks are manufacturing the Transports. Soften the bay's defenses with the Elite Cannon Galleons, and then lay into the Transports with your Heavy Demolition Ships and Fast Fire Ships. You'll knock out most of the Transports.

This will hinder but not stop the Turks. They'll continue to build Transports even if you raze all their Docks. Curious, no? No matter, constantly reinforce your forward fleet—you might even build a Dock on the Turkish shore to speed the reinforcement's arrival.

Although your best efforts will not hold all the Turks at bay, they'll decrease the number of Turks that reach

> **Tip:** *Despite your fleet's proximity to the Turks, it's still a good idea to station a handful of Heavy Demolition Ships in front of your coast (as shown in Figure 9-16). Those Turkish Transports are fast, and you never can tell when a couple will break through your forward fleet.*

> **Tip:** *Concentrate on training troops that use your excess resources. For example, if you have plenty of Wood and Food but are short on Gold, buy Pikemen and Elite Skirmishers.*

your shores. Sprinkling Heavy Demolition Ships next to your coast will reduce them even more. Those that do survive will be easily eliminated by your ground troops, and you will win.

Manzikert

Objectives:

Figure 9-16   *Heavy Demolition Ships await the Turkish invader.*

- Receive tributes from the Theme of Galatia by capturing their Town Center.
- Receive tributes from the Theme of Pisidia by capturing their Town Center.
- Receive tributes from the Theme of Cappadocia by capturing their Town Center.
- Defeat the Byzantine army.
- Destroy the four Saracen Towers so that your allies can mine their Gold. (Optional)

Hints:

- Your Turkish army has no Villagers. To replenish your troops, you'll need to rely on tributes from conquered Byzantine Themes.
- Do not destroy many buildings of the Byzantine Themes or you'll have less to use once they're conquered.
- This battle takes place centuries before the discovery of gunpowder.
- Garrisoned Battering Rams are useful for taking out gates and towers.

Scout Reports:

- The Seljuk Turk army (purple) is far from home and does not have the resources to construct a base. You can, however, train additional units.
- Additional resources and buildings can be gained by conquering the three Byzantine Themes (towns) of Cappadocia, Pisidia, and Galatia and the Saracen (cyan) Gold mines. However, you must defeat—not conquer—the Byzantine army.
- The Byzantine Themes rely largely on walls and towers for defense. The Byzantine army is a different story. You can expect to combat Cataphracts, Monks, and the famous Roman Legions.

Note: *The Byzantines will frequently send a raiding party against you and your newfound allies. Fight them at the second set of gates (as shown in Figure 9-17). By doing so, the Cappadocian Watch Towers will add the weight of their arrows to your defense.*

First Walkthrough: Hey Diddle Diddle, Go Right Up the Middle

The key to this walkthrough is moving your units straight up the center of the map. Let's get started. Lasso all your units, and head out of your base. Build three Rams and as many Knights as your money allows, and trace the valley to the gates of Cappadocia. Attack the gates with your troops. When the Cappadocians respond, draw them out of the gates and slaughter them. Once the Cappadocian camels are eliminated, destroy the gates with the Rams.

Figure 9-17   *The Watch Towers take the edge off the Byzantine attack.*

Bring down the Watch Tower east of the gates, and then attack the next set of gates. Continue through the third set, and follow the road to the Town Center, which is nestled inside the Palisade walls. Move a unit next to the Town Center to convert the Cappadocians to your cause.

With the Cappadocians subdued, it's time to research new technology. Use the Cappadocian Blacksmith to research Barding Armor, and take advantage of all the upgrades offered at the Stable, Barracks, and Archery Range. Once the upgrades are researched, it's time to head to Pisidia. Exit Cappadocia, and approach Pisidia's outer gate. Assault it with your mounted troops, holding some Swordsmen and Crossbowmen in reserve. Pisidia usually responds with several Onagers. Allow the Onagers to engage your troops, and then retreat. Unbelievably, the Onagers will follow you, leaving behind the safety of their city.

Swarm and destroy the Onagers. Use the Ram to knock down the gate, and advance toward the main city gate. You won't, however, need to attack this gate. If you take down the Watch Tower to the right of the gate, you can squeeze through some Light Cavalry. After they squirt through, send them northeast to the Town Hall (as shown in Figure 9-18). That's two down and two to go.

Build seven Battering Rams. Fill three of them with Long Swordsmen. Keep a healthy reserve of Crossbowmen and Light Cavalry. Send the Battering Rams against the gates of Galatia. The Galatians will respond with Scorpions and Monks, but the Rams will carry the day and crash the gate. After they do, release the Long Swordsmen to create a diversion while your Light Cavalry heads due north to liberate the Galatia Town Center.

Figure 9-18 *Capturing the Pisidian Town Center places you on the road to victory.*

With Galatia under foot, it's time to upgrade your Long Swordsmen to Two-Handed Swordsmen, upgrade your Cavalry Archers to Heavy Cavalry Archers—research Parthian Tactics, too—and build a sizable army, including Trebuchets. Be sure to include a little bit of everything in your army: Knights, Pikemen, Two-Handed Swordsmen, Crossbowmen, and Heavy Cavalry Archers.

Advance toward the eastern corner of the map. Stay well ahead of your Trebuchets. There are Byzantines about, and you want to clear some of them before bringing the Trebuchets into play. There are two ponds in the eastern part of the map. A Castle waits south of the westernmost of the two. Once the Castle is spotted, attack it with your Trebuchets. This should bring all the Byzantines patrolling the area down on you. That's okay; slaughter them, and destroy the Castle.

East of the Castle is the gate leading to the heart of Byzantine. Take it out with the Trebuchets, eliminating any Byzantines that respond with your army. Once through the gate, follow the road—there's another gate that you'll have to destroy—to the Byzantine Town Center, destroy it, and you win.

Second Walkthrough: The Shortcut

As is sometimes the case, the second walkthrough is similar to the first. On the other hand, if you're challenged for time, this is the walkthrough for you. Begin as before, storming the Cappadocia gates (as shown in Figure 9-19). Once Cappadocia is secured, upgrade and expand your army.

Figure 9-19 *Start your invasion by smashing these gates.*

Aim your expansion at Battering Rams and Light Cavalry. Make six Battering Rams and 10–15 Light Cavalry. Sneak the Battering Rams and Cavalry past the southeast corner of Pisidia, fighting off any advances by the Byzantines with your ponies. Assault Galatia's main gate with the Rams. Once the gate collapses, send the Light Cavalry north to Galatia's Town Center (as shown in Figure 9-20). Now put together a slightly smaller version of the Byzantine assault army mentioned in the first walkthrough.

March your army east, and assault Byzantine. If you've been quick enough, you'll find that the town falls quite easily and you'll win.

Figure 9-20   *The Galatia Town Center is stop number two on the road to victory.*

Note: *Make no mistake, you won't have as powerful an army as the one that you assaulted Byzantine with in the first walkthrough, but the Byzantines won't have as much time to prepare for your assault. Life's full of trade-offs.*

Tip: *You might find it difficult to build an army capable of defeating the Byzantines with the contributions from only Galatia and Cappadocia. Accordingly, you might want to bring down the four Saracen towers in the western corner of the map or return to and capture Pisidia. Either act will increase your resources.*

Morayang

Objectives:

- Prevent the Japanese from destroying Korea's Wonder. (Optional)
- Defend Korea from the Japanese.

Hints:

- Defend the Wonder if you can, but you can win without it.
- The Japanese navy is superior to the Korean navy. You'll need to devise a way to even the odds.
- The Koreans are initially unable to construct Castles or train some of their most powerful units.

Scout Reports:

- Korea (red) has an extensive town, but the Koreans are vulnerable to the Japanese navy, particularly the Cannon Galleons.
- Expect the Japanese (yellow) to attack with everything that they have, including ships and Samurai on Transports. Play defensively until you have the means to bring the battle back to the Japanese homeland.
- You have two potential allies: Admiral Yi (green) is a brilliant Korean tactician who will certainly assist—provided that you locate him. The Chinese (orange) are no friends of Korea, but they fear the Japanese even more. They might be of assistance.

First Walkthrough: One if by Land

Pause the game, select all your warships, and send them north to attack the Japanese fleet. Dispatch five Villagers to the bridge north of your Wonder, and

research Hand Cart. Build a gate across your end of the bridge, and extend a Stone Wall to either side of it. Build a couple of Bombard Towers and a Keep (as shown in Figure 9-21).

The Japanese raiders will storm your defenses, but you should be able to hold. Once you've beaten back the attack, build a Siege Workshop and construct a Battering Ram. Bring up some Swordsmen and Light Cavalry to escort the Battering Ram across

Figure 9-21 *These defenses will weather the toughest Japanese attack.*

the bridge. Take down the Guard Tower on the other side of the bridge. Once it's down, mount a Light Cavalry in the Transport—there's one waiting on the shore—and cross the river.

Ride southwest until you find Admiral Yi's base. Enter the base, and Admiral Yi will join your team. It's a welcome addition, because he brings three TurtleShips with him. Use the ships to clear the remaining Japanese from your coast.

Note: *The Japanese will still sneak some troops ashore. It's a good idea to have a reserve of troops to attack any incursion. Knights and Cavalry Archers do the job well. They can quickly respond to incursions and are strong enough to seal off the incursors.*

Tip: *Shadow your army's movement with a strong naval force consisting of Turtles and Fire Ships. These can bombard targets from the sea, which will hasten their destruction.*

Tip: *Although the TurtleShips have awesome armor, their cannon has a limited range. The Cannon Galleons are much more effective against the Japanese Keeps and Bombard Towers.*

Now it's time to go after the Japanese Docks. They have seven sprinkled up their coast. Two of those seven are actually on inland waterways leading from the coast. Build a fleet of four TurtleShips and five Fire Ships, and head south from the Korean Docks. You'll soon find a peninsula capped with a Dock. Axe the Dock, and then follow the water around the southern end of the map. There you'll find the second Dock.

After eliminating these two, land your ground forces where you found the first Dock. Build a couple of Bombard Towers—the Koreans are good at that—and ship over a pair of Trebuchets from Yi's Castle. This will clear this end of the map. Construct an Archery Range and Barracks. Build a sizable force (as shown in Figure 9-22), and march north up the Japanese stretch of land.

Flow north, protecting your Trebuchets with your infantry. The

Figure 9-22   *This is the type of army that you'll need to win the mission.*

Trebuchets outrange anything the Japanese have, so they can fire with impunity—as long as you keep them safe from marauding Samurai. After you destroy the last Dock, the game will end.

Second Walkthrough: Two if by Sea

The first walkthrough featured a combined arms offensive, with the glory shared in equal part by the army and navy. This walkthrough, however, stresses a nautical solution. Begin the mission as before. Continue until you have access to Yi's TurtleShips (as shown in Figure 9-23). Use these (and whatever Fire Ships you can afford to build) to sweep your coast of the Japanese. Once the coast is clear, so to speak, you might take your fleet to the Japanese homeland. Begin with the southernmost Dock, and slowly work your way north.

Figure 9-23   *These TurtleShips mark the mission's turning tide.*

Tip: *The Chinese army are great for protecting your Dock. That way you don't have to worry about building your own.*

Figure 9-24   *Building a Dock on the Japanese coast cuts down the time it takes your reinforcements to arrive.*

Use your Cannon Galleons to take down the Japanese Keeps. On the other hand, the Galleons need the protection of Turtle Ships and Fire Ships to survive. Once you've cleared the two southernmost Docks (one on the beach and one in the inlet), build a Dock of your own (as shown in Figure 9-24). Continue to crank out the ships, and move north. You can destroy every Dock from the sea. Do so, and victory will be yours.

Tours

Objectives:

- Prevent the Moslems from destroying any of your three Town Centers.
- Capture the six Trade Carts in the Moor's baggage train, and bring them to the cathedral in Tours.

Hints:

- The Moslems are attacking outlying Frankish farms. This will slow them down while you send for Charles Martel's army and build up your defenses.
- The Berbers and Moors use inexpensive troops in combat. While Frank Knights can defeat them, the Moslems spend fewer of their resources fielding armies.
- You can click signs for directions.

Scout Reports:

- The Frank (red) army defends the large city of Tours to the north. Charles Martel's army is to the south of the city.
- There are two armies of Moslems: The Berbers (yellow) occupy the western edge of the map. They train Light Cavalry, Swordsmen, and Rams, but their town is not well defended and could fall to an early attack. The Moors (green) have occupied the city of Poitiers to the southwest, making their army harder to defeat. They train Camels, Knights, and Scorpions but will switch to Mamelukes given enough time.

First Walkthrough: First Come, First Serve

The key to this first walkthrough is simple: eliminate the Berbers. Once the number of your enemies is cut in half, it's fairly easy to win the game. Begin by lassoing Martel's army and sending them against the Berbers, who are located in the middle of the southwest border of the map. The first objective is the Berber's Town Center. Swarm it with all your warriors (as shown in Figure 9-25).

Both the Berbers and Moors will mount counterattacks. Keep your troops together, and try to anchor a flank against a building or trees as you fight the Arabs. You might also want to train some Pikemen and send them to help. Once the Town Center is destroyed,

Note: *Your Villagers should be eagerly gathering resources. You'll want to crank out five or six Villagers in addition to the starting allotment. Don't forget to research Hand Cart either.*

Figure 9-25   *Charles Martel's army attacks the Berber's Town Center.*

Note: *If you're playing on the Advanced (or higher) level of difficulty, the Moors will constantly mount attacks against Tours. Keeps (garrisoned with Archers), Pikemen, and Horse Archers work well in fending off these incursions. The Keeps wear down the Moors, the Pikemen kill any that breach your walls, and the Horse Archers sally forth against the Scorpions.*

Note: *By now, the Moors might have axed one of the Trade Carts. Who knows why, but they do it. If so, you'll have to go for the complete destruction of the Moors.*

take out the other military buildings (Barracks, Stables, and so on). When they fall, so do the Berbers.

Continue to buff your economy, and advance to the Castle Age as soon as possible. Bring a Villager or two to the site of the Berber's village, and construct a Siege Engine Workshop and a Town Center.

After the Town Center is finished, train eight Villagers and set them to work mining the Gold, chopping the Wood, and farming the land found near the Berber Village. It's not a bad idea to build three Keeps and a medium-sized army; the Moors won't sit on their hands while you assemble your buildings and army.

Advance to the Imperial Age; research Chemistry; and build a pair of Trebuchets, three Bombard Cannons, a couple of Battering Rams, and 10–15 Hand Cannoneers. Attack the Moor base, destroy the Town Center and military structures (as shown in Figure 9-26), including the Blacksmith, and you'll win.

Figure 9-26 *The Franks are razing the Moors' town.*

Second Walkthrough: Capturing the Carts

This walkthrough is simple. If you can pull it off, you'll win the mission quickly. Select Charles Martel's army, and move them southwest to Poitiers. When you arrive at the wall, attack the east gate (as shown in Figure 9-27).

You'll rarely have to destroy the gate. A Moor Knight or Villager will come through it, and your troops can pour into the Moor compound. Select one of your Knights, and direct him to the Trade Carts, which wait on the west edge of the camp. Order the rest of your entourage to battle the camp's inhabitants.

Figure 9-27   *You won't have to beat on the east gate long before someone opens it.*

Note: *When playing Advanced or higher difficulty, it's nearly impossible to overcome the Moor defenders. There are too many, and they are too aggressive. In this case, your best bet is to attempt to draw them away from the lone Knight sent to capture the Trade Carts and hope for the best.*

Figure 9-28   *The Trade Carts arrive at the Cathedral.*

Once the Knight captures the Trade Carts, send the carts north to the Cathedral in Tours. Leave a rear guard consisting of Throwing Axemen, and retreat the rest of your Cavalry toward Tours. The Cavalry will form the Trade Cart's escorts. Take them to the Cathedral (as shown in Figure 9-28), and the mission will end.

Vindlandsaga

Objectives:

- Erik the Red must survive.
- Transport Erik the Red west across the ocean to the New World, and establish a colony there.
- Construct a Town Center, Market, and 12 Houses on the shores of the New World.
- Did we mention that Erik must survive?

Hints:

- Resources in Norway will run out soon. You must colonize other lands to keep the Viking civilization prosperous.

- Skalds tells of an ocean where worms eat away at the hulls of ships.
- The Vikings can advance to the Castle Age only.

Scout Reports:

- The Vikings under Erik the Red (red) have few buildings and only a handful of Berserks to defend themselves from ravenous wolves. Although you're safe from attack for the moment, Vikings from Greenland might raid your shores.
- The British (blue) have little in the way of a standing army, so they're ripe for raiding.
- Greenland (green) is more of a mystery, but it is known that the Vikings there have many Longships.
- A race of wildmen (purple) are rumored to live in the New World.

First Walkthrough: Side-Stepping Greenland

Build a Lumber Camp, and order the three Villagers to chop Wood. Train more Villagers, and move them southwest. You'll find some deer and fishing holes near the coast. Build a Mill, hunt the deer, and fish the fish. As soon as you're able, build a Dock and construct five Fishing ships. There's food near your coast and in the sea to the west. Once you reach 500 Food, advance to the Feudal Age.

Build another Dock and two Barracks (as shown in Figure 9-29). You'll

Figure 9-29 *These are the buildings you'll need to support your invasion of England.*

Note: *Villagers are key to the early part of the game. You'll need at least 12 to gather enough Wood and Food. The more, however, the better.*

Note: *You must be quick about this; the Greenland Vikings will soon send raiding parties. If you're playing Standard mode, you'll begin with a Castle. That makes it much easier to fend off the Greenland Vikings. Not only will the Castle defenses take down the Greenlander Berserkers, but also once you advance to the Castle Age, the Build Longboat option pops in the Dock build queue. If, however, you selected the Advanced setting (or higher), you must build a Castle—a Stone deposit waits in the east corner of the map—to access the Longboats needed to defeat the Greenlanders' nautical overtures.*

Tip: *The Spearmen are particularly valuable in this mission. Yes, they have an effective attack, but more importantly, they cost no Gold. On the other hand, neither do the Pikemen, but you'll face no Cavalry, so their value is debatable.*

Note: *Once the towers—and any Greenlanders that come to their aid—fall, march north, keeping the forest on your left shoulder. Actually, it's not on your shoulder. That would be very uncomfortable. That's what we gamers-turned-writers call an allegory. I now return you to your regularly scheduled walkthrough.*

need these to support your invasion of England. Load three Transports with Spearman, Erik, the Berserks, Man-at-Arms, and a couple of Villagers. Sail west to the British coast.

Defeat the British Archers, and destroy the Keep, Town Center, and Market to reap your golden reward. Establish a new base, and gather the resources to advance to the Castle Age.

Once you've subdued the poor Britons and collected the 1700 Gold their conquest provides, upgrade your warrior's armor, attack, and arrow-flinging capabilities. Assemble a task force of Crossbowmen, Spearmen, Long Swordsmen, Villagers, and Erik. Shove them in a few Transports, and escort them with six Longboats and three War Galleys.

Sail due north from England. The New World, baseball, and hamburgers wait to the west, but the clever folks at Ensemble have placed a solid barrier of shoals that will wreck any ship attempting to traverse the ocean between England and North America. (Strange, they weren't there when Columbus set sail.) North lies Greenland; you'll probably hit the beach near a pair of Keeps. Attack them with your army and the War Galleys (as shown in Figure 9-30). Use the Longboats to take out the Dock a bit northeast of the site.

You'll find Gold in Greenland's interior. Set up defenses here and a Dock, Archery Range, and Barracks on the west coast. Mine the Gold. Build some Transports, and reinforce your army. (Make it a bit Archer-heavy.) When ready, sail northwest to the New World.

On arrival, place your warriors in a line formation and advance inland a bit. Stop when the first Skraelings attack. These folks are all Woad Raiders and Militia. The trick is to

Figure 9-30 *The War Galleys work quite well at dismantling Guard Towers, thank you.*

pin-cushion them with arrows. A line (or box, for that matter) formation protects your Crossbowman while their quills work their deadly magic on the ravenous Skraelings.

Put the Villagers to work constructing the required Town Center, Market, and 12 homes. It goes without saying that the Town Center is job number one. With the Town Center completed, you can crank out as many Villagers as needed to rapidly complete your urban renewal project and win the mission.

Second Walkthrough: Head to Head

The first walkthrough is a fun and an exciting way to win the mission. It does, however, have a problem—you never eliminate the Greenland Vikings. Hence, they just keep on coming. It's no fun to

Note: *I feel the first walkthrough works best when playing Standard. This walkthrough works best at Advanced or higher.*

simultaneously fight Skraeling Woad Raiders while beating Greenland Berserkers away from your Gold. This walkthrough solves that problem but takes a bit more time to win.

Begin as before, but—as Yoda would say—build not your Man-at-Arms nor any other Gold-sucking entity. Rapidly advance to the Feudal Age and then, using the Gold not spent on Men-at-Arms, the Castle Age.

Now send your Transports laden with a Skirmisher/Pikeman/Erik/Berserker army to pay the English a visit (as shown in Figure 9-31).

Rapidly capture the Briton Gold, and begin spewing Longboats from your Docks. Search and destroy the main Greenland fleet, upgrade your warriors, churn out some Berserkers from the Castles, load them all on Transports, and move north to Greenland. Take down the two Guard Towers, and move inland as described in the first walkthrough. Now, however, build a Castle, Barracks, Archery Range, Stable, and a fistful of Guard Towers to protect them. Churn out

Figure 9-31   *The Vikings head for their inevitable confrontation with their Greenland brethren.*

Note: *You'll need to simultaneously construct a Transport fleet and Skirmisher/ Pikeman army. And remember, if you're playing Advanced, you'll want to locate that Stone deposit in the east and construct a Castle.*

some Light Cavalry, and send them north to disrupt the Greenlanders' economy.

Slowly march your footsoldiers (a combination of Long Swordsmen, Crossbowmen, and Berserkers) up the

center of Greenland, destroying every-thing in their path. When you reach the Greenland Castle, train about 10 Petards. You have no siege weapons, and Petards are your next best bet. Assault the Castle with everything you have. Once the Castle engages your warriors, send the Petards to the rear of the structure to get in their licks. The Castle will soon fall and with it the Vikings of Greenland.

Once Greenland is conquered, build Transports on the west coast, ferry your army to the New World, and slash and construct as enumerated in the previous walkthrough. Once the colony is established, you'll win.

> **Tip:** *Light Cavalry are excellent Villager hunters. They have an extensive line of sight, they're fast, and they're plenty strong enough to quickly eliminate a Villager. If you kill enough Villagers, the Greenlanders won't be able to make any more Berserkers. That's a good thing.*

> **Note:** *You must destroy the Vikings' Town Center, Castle, and military buildings to eliminate them as opponents.*

Chapter Ten

ALTERNATE EMPIRES: IN-DEPTH STRATEGIES FOR MASTERING THE NEW GAME TYPES

Whether you play against the computer or battle your friends on The Zone, a variety of game types keeps the fun going with a mix of different strategies and objectives. *The Age of Kings* provided several game types for your enjoyment. *Microsoft Age of Empires II: The Conquerors Expansion* further enhances your RTS pleasure by offering three new game styles for Empire builders. A total of seven game types are now available:

- **Random Map**   As a gamer, you can choose from four victory types. A *Standard* setting enables you to win in one of three ways: by conquest, by holding all of the Relics for 300 years, or by building a Wonder and preventing other civilizations from razing it within a certain amount of time. In *Conquest* matches, you must destroy your opponent's entire population, military structures (except towers and walls), and all technology-related buildings. *Time Limit* battles end when the time expires (the civilization/team with the highest score wins) or when one civilization/team conquers all the others. *Score* matches end when a civilization/team reaches the required score or when a civilization/team conquers all the others.
- **Regicide**   Think of this game as an *Age of Empires II* version of chess. You and your opponents start with a King, a Castle, and some Villagers. The goal is to protect your crowned dude from harm's way while you kill the opponent's monarch. Long live your King—because once your sovereign bites the dust, you're ousted from the contest.

- **Death Match**   All civilizations/teams begin this game with large stock-piles of Wood, Food, Gold, and Stone. Although you must gather resources, the emphasis is on building and fighting. In a slugfest to the death, the last civilization/team standing wins.
- **Scenario...**   The fun doesn't stop. You can battle opponents on more *Age of Empires II* maps or play on a map you or one of your friends designs.
- **King of the Hill**   This popular real-time strategy game is now part of *Age of Empires II*. This time, though, the "hill" is a Monument located in the center of the map. Simply put, the civilization/team that possesses this structure the longest wins.
- **Wonder Race**   Economic efficiency, always important, is even more critical in these matches. The first person to erect a Wonder wins. Thus, you must know how to use your resources wisely and advance quickly through the Ages.
- **Defend the Wonder**   One civilization/team must defend a ready-built Wonder, complete with surrounding walls, from attacking opponents for a specified amount of time.

> **Note:** *Check out Chapter 17 in* Microsoft Age of Empires II: The Age of Kings: Inside Moves, *the official Microsoft guide for strategies and tips on Random Map, Regicide, and Death Match scenarios.*

King of the Hill, Wonder Race, and Defend the Wonder are the new additions to *Age of Empires II*. This chapter is devoted solely to basic strategies for these game types.

No simple one-strategy-fits-all magic formula exists for winning these new games—*Age of Empires II* is too complex for that. You must always take a number of variables into account, including the following:

- The type of map you're playing on (mostly water, all land, or quite a bit of both) and the amount and type of resources located there
- The starting location of your civilization on the map
- The civilization you're playing as and the civilization you're teaming up with
- The civilizations you're playing against
- The number of opponents you're battling, and whether they're teaming up against you
- The difficulty level of the game's artificial intelligence
- Your experience level and the experience level of your opponents

To become a good player, you must be familiar with the different civilizations and maps. Another key to winning is learning the game's hot key combinations. The basic strategies for the King of the Hill, Wonder Race, and Defend the Wonder game types are just that—basic strategies. In other words, these are the bare necessities for winning these games. The following sections provide you with some tips and notes for dealing with specific situations that might arise during these contests.

Basic King of the Hill Tactics

The objective in King of the Hill games is simple: control the Monument for the longest period of time and you win. Monuments are located in the center of the map. Sometimes they're on an island if an island is in the map's center; sometimes they're partly surrounded by cliffs or trees; and sometimes no barrier of any sort surrounds them. Defending the Monument with Stone Walls and towers is a must. It's often necessary to use siege weapons when you're trying to capture the Monument. The easiest civilizations to command in King of the Hill matches are those with adequate defenses and economic strength—generally the Byzantines, Celts, Mongols, Persians, Spanish, Teutons, and Turks.

> **Note:** *Forgetting to defend the Town Center is one of the biggest mistakes novice King of the Hill players make. Often players concentrate so hard on taking or protecting the Monument that they neglect their original settlement. Don't do this! Doing so leaves your Town Center and resources open to attack.*

The Dark Age

Use your Scout Cavalry or Eagle Warrior to explore the map and cut through the fog (if your environment is not 100 percent visible), and locate resources and the enemy's site. Meanwhile, have one of your Villagers erect several Houses while the others herd Sheep and Wild Turkeys. (See Figure 10-1.) Churn out more Villagers at the Town Center. Use several of them to chop Wood, after placing a Lumber Camp near a large forest. Food and Wood, with emphasis on the former, are the most important resources, especially in the opening seconds of the game.

> **Tip:** *Use your Eagle Warrior to deplete your opponent's Sheep, Wild Turkeys, and Deer, especially if your enemy already herded these animals into his or her Town Center. Slaughtering the animals reduces your opponent's access to easy Food sources. Furthermore, the Eagle Warrior is quicker than Villagers— and even the Scout Cavalry—so he should be able to escape if attacked.*

Figure 10-1   *Sheep or Wild Turkeys should always be your first Food resource. Unlike Wild Boar, these animals do not fight back. Furthermore, they do not require Wood (as Farms do).*

After exploring the territory, navigate your Scout Cavalry or Eagle Warrior to the Monument. Often when you play against the computer, you can get an early foothold on the Monument with this tactic. However, it's possible only if the Monument is not on another island. If that's the case, you have to wait until the Feudal Age when Transport Ships become available. Flesh-and-blood opponents, on the other hand, might counter early with their Scout Cavalry or Eagle Warrior. In this case, a fight to the finish might take place between the two units. An Eagle Warrior is nice to have in such situations because of his superiority over the Scout Cavalry.

Tip: *Always construct a Dock in the Dark Age if you're on a map with lots of water. First, you can churn out Fishing Ships to help bring in Food. Second, you can gain control of the rivers and seas before your opponents do. If the Monument is on an island, Transport Ships are important to your mission. Don't wait until you have Galleons to take the Monument from an opponent; if you do, your opponent will have plenty of defenses there by then to keep you—excuse the pun—at bay.*

For the most part, you want to concentrate on your economy in the opening Age. Often the two Dark Age buildings of choice are the Lumber Camp and Mill. They offer resource-gathering improvements through new technologies and decreased walking distance for your Villagers. For additional defenses, it's a good idea to build a Barracks near the Monument. However, erecting one on the outskirts of any enemy settlement is better. This strategy enables you to attack your opponent's Villagers, Lumber

Camps, and Mills with greater ease. In turn, it depletes your opponent's resources and thwarts him or her from mounting an effective offensive strategy on the Monument.

> **Note:** *Building Palisade Walls and stationing Militia near the Monument is not the best way to defend your possession. Always remember that the best defense is a good offense. Consistently attacking your opponents is the most effective way to keep them from going after the Monument.*

The Feudal Age

The Feudal Age requires more resources, so order your Villagers to exploit Gold and Stone sites. Erect more Houses—unless you're playing as the Huns, in which case you'll need the ad-

ditional hands. Build Mining Camps near two or more Gold and Stone sites (as shown in Figure 10-2). Place Towers near these points to prevent enemy Villagers from scouring the area. Build more Lumber Camps, too. For Food, continue taking down Wild Boar, collecting Forage Berries, and sowing Farms.

Attack your opponent, especially if you haven't done so yet. Build an Archery Range and Stable near the Monument. Sift Archers, Skirmishers, and Scout Cavalry

Figure 10-2   *Building a Mining Camp between two mining sites enables Villagers to exploit both mines with more efficiency.*

along with upgraded Barracks units into enemy settlements. Concentrate on attacking peripheral buildings (those on the kingdom outskirts) and Villagers. Also, don't forget to defend the Monument and Town Center. Allocate military

Note: *Often building a Blacksmith—instead of a Stable—works best in this Age. Stables can produce only Scout Cavalry at this time. The Barracks' Man-at-Arms is as durable as the mounted unit and can dish out more Attack Points. Moreover, a Blacksmith is necessary for Infantry and Archer technology and is a prerequisite for the Siege Workshop, a building you'll definitely need later. Constructing a Market is a good idea when playing on a Team.*

units to both locations. If you control the Monument, set up a Stone Wall around it, and construct walls and Watch Towers at choke holes.

The Castle Age

Resource gathering should require less micromanaging at this stage. Mine Gold and Stone, for you need both heavily during this time. Continue building Farms near the Town Center and Mills, and erect a few more Lumber Camps near forests. Churn out additional Villagers.

Creating another Town Center helps in this endeavor. Do not erect it near your original Town Center. Instead, place it near the Monument or a forest. You should have at least two settlements; you don't want opponents to assault a village and destroy both Town Centers in one attack.

Tip: *To weaken an opponent's grasp on the Monument, attack structures that implicitly affect his or her civilization's economic well being. Go for Mills, Lumber Camps, and Mining Camps. If you have incredible success, go for the Town Center. Putting a damper on your opponent's economy affects his or her military strength.*

The Castle and Siege Workshop are the two buildings of choice during the Castle Age. Erect both of these near the Monument. Sprinkle Guard Towers around both for defense. Attack your opponent's settlement with unique units, as well as upgraded Stable and Archery Range units. Remember to place some of these units near the Monument for defenses. If you need to capture the Monument, create a horde of Mangonels and Battering Rams, and defend them with other units. Use the siege weapons to raze walls and towers. Send in a wave of Stable and Archery Range units to flush the Monument and gain control of it.

The Imperial Age

While you preserve your economy (which should require little hands-on maintenance), attack your enemy with unique units, cavalry, siege weapons, Trebuchets, and—if applicable—Cannon Galleons. Use Monks to convert important enemy buildings such as Castles, Docks, Stables, and Siege Workshops. The Spanish Missionaries are quite adept at conversions. A group of them can

wreak havoc on a settlement. The Korean Turtle Ships are strong in water-based maps, especially when the Monument is situated on an island. Overall, you must continually mount assaults and research technologies to be competitive during this stage of the game.

Basic Wonder Race Tactics

Wonder Race scenarios strictly emphasize economic strategy. Combat is not allowed, so you can't use military units to destroy your opponent's structures. Victory involves efficiently and quickly advancing to the Imperial Age so you can be the first to complete a Wonder. Without relying on military strength, you'll need to follow three general strategies to win Wonder Races:

- Build economic structures—not military-related edifices.
- Research technologies that improve your economy.
- Create sufficient Villagers to gather resources.

These are the essentials. Although every civilization has specific areas in which it's economically proficient (some more than others), all civilizations are capable of winning these matches. (Novices will find that commanding the Saracens and Teutons requires more effort, though.) Success depends primarily on the map type, the amount and kinds of resources, and your skill. The following walkthrough will assist you in the latter department.

The Dark Age

Use your Scout Cavalry or Eagle Warrior to explore your surroundings and evaporate the fog (if it's on). Have all but one of your Villagers gather Food, concentrating at first on Sheep and Wild Turkeys. The remaining Villager should build a few Houses and then chop down the trees nearest the Town Center. As soon as your Wood supply reaches 100, erect a Lumber Camp adjacent to the closest forest.

Meanwhile, churn out more Villagers at the Town Center. Send them to cut Wood near the Lumber Camp and gather more Food. Construct a Mill near a Deer herd (as shown in Figure 10-3) to decrease the distance your Hunters must walk; rather than having to traverse back to the Town Center, they can take care of business in just a few steps. While your

> **Note:** *The Aztecs, Britons, Celts, Goths, Huns, Japanese, Mongols, Persians, and Spanish are some of the strongest civilizations economically during the Dark Age.*

Figure 10-3 *Placing a Mill near Deer provides your Hunters with a close meat drop-off point.*

Hunters finish off the Wild Boar and Deer, have several Villagers sow Farms. Also, erect a Mining Camp near at least two mines (preferably one each of Stone and Gold). Place four Villagers at the Gold Mine and two at the Stone Mine; this gives you an early—but modest—start on these resources. As soon as you have 500 Food, research the Feudal Age. By this time, you should have created at least 25 to 30 Villagers.

The Feudal Age

Create more Villagers and build more Houses, and concentrate on Food and Wood. As soon as you have 250 Food and 175 Wood, research these three technologies: the Wheelbarrow (Town Center), Horse Collar (Mill), and Double-Bit Axe (Lumber Camp). Build a Blacksmith and a Market. Locate some more mines, and build another Mining Camp in their vicinity. Also, research Gold Mining and Stone Mining at the Mining Camps.

> **Note:** *The Aztecs, Celts, Chinese, Franks, Goths, Japanese, Mayans, Mongols, and Vikings sport the best economic advantages in the Feudal Age.*

As soon as you have 800 Food and 200 Gold, research the Castle Age. You should have created a total of 35 to 40 Villagers since the beginning of the game.

The Castle Age

Churn out enough Villagers to push your total to at least 50. Build a couple of Houses, sow more Farms, and continue chopping Wood. Research the Hand Cart (Town Center), Bow Saw (Lumber Camp), and Heavy Plow (Mill). Next, research Gold Shaft Mining and Stone Shaft Mining, a task that's easier if you already have two Mining Camps. Make sure that you have at least twice as many Miners as you did in the previous Age, preferably 12 to 20. Next, build a Monastery and a University. Whatever you do, don't waste resources on a Castle. (See Figure 10-4.) As soon as you have 1000 Food and 800 Gold, research the Imperial Age.

> **Note:** *The Aztecs, Byzantines, Celts, Chinese, Koreans, Mongols, Persians, Turks, and Vikings have economic advantages during the Castle Age.*

Figure 10-4   *Don't build any Castles if you're planning to win a Wonder Race; they're a huge economic drain!*

The Imperial Age

You need 1000 Wood, 1000 Gold, and 1000 Stone. Disband all farming, and allocate Farmers to Lumberjacking and Mining duties. How you distribute Farmers, of course, depends on which resources are most needed. If you have several hundred fewer units of Gold than Wood, place more Farmers on Gold Mines and send fewer to help the Lumberjacks. Don't waste resources researching Crop Rotation, only the Two-Man Saw (if necessary). As soon as you have enough resources to build a Wonder, assign all of your Villagers to construct it. This improves your building speed.

Basic Defend the Wonder Tactics

Defend the Wonder matches set players up in the Imperial Age. All available technologies for your civilization are researched. A huge stockpile of resources is in your hands. Player 1 has a Town Center and a Wonder surrounded by a wall (as shown in Figure 10-5). Other players have a Town Center encased by a wall. All you have to do—depending on the role you take—is attack or defend.

Figure 10-5 *Player 1 begins the match in good shape. The trick is staying that way.*

Of course, there's more to playing Defend the Wonder than that. This section will help you get started by providing a general overview of key details and basic strategies. You'll learn the best and most efficient ways to destroy or protect a Wonder. Read on, and you'll be on your way to victory.

Defending the Wonder

Civilizations with efficient economies, decent armies, and strong defenses fare best when in this role. In general, the Britons, Byzantines, Chinese, Franks, Koreans, Mayans, Teutons, and Turks are the best civilizations for defending a Wonder. The following are necessary strategies for defenders:

- Place towers and a Castle near your Wonder.
- Place Trebuchets and Monks just inside your Fortified Walls for the farthest reach from inside your kingdom.

- Erect towers in choke points, such as marshes and gaps between Fortified Walls and forests.
- Create plenty of Villagers and use them to gather resources; concentrate heavily on Stone, a necessary component of most defenses.
- Locate Gold and Stone sites just outside your village's walls. Build Mining Camps there with Fortified Walls surrounding the area.
- Build another Town Center to help churn out more Villagers.
- Create several groups of armies to defend the Wonder and attack key enemy economic sites, such as Mills, Lumber Camps, and Mining Camps.
- Garrison troops inside structures. This is always a good idea: First of all, buildings provide protection. Second, you can trick your attacker into thinking that your settlement has few mobile defenses. With his or her army confidently rushing in with fewer units than usual, you can then ambush your attacker with your garrisoned forces.
- Dispatch an army or navy to assault the enemy's settlement as they begin attacking your village.

Attacking the Wonder

Civilizations with strong armies and powerful siege equipment work well for attacking Wonders. The Celts, Goths, Huns, Mongols, Persians, Saracens, Spanish, and Vikings are the best civilizations for this task. The following are critical strategies for capturing Wonders:

- Erect a Town Center and towers near the enemy settlement. The closer you are to the enemy, the better. Not only can you keep a close eye on developments, you can also prevent the opponent from gathering Stone and Gold outside of his or her village and use them for your units instead. Taking control of the map is one of the first steps toward victory.
- Build a Siege Workshop, Archery Range, and Stable near your opponent's kingdom. The less distance your military units have to travel, the more time you save in your race against the clock. Just be sure to place a gate and a wall around these structures.
- Use siege weapons, Trebuchets, and Galleons to raze enemy units in this order: military units and towers, military structures, and economic structures such as Farms and Camps. Always weaken your opponent's

economy and military forces before you attack the Wonder. If you don't, he or she can rebuild forces and a "wounded" Wonder, which in turn forces you to waste more time mounting additional attacks. Don't forget to garrison infantry and foot Archers in Rams for additional support.

- Attack the enemy village simultaneously from multiple points. For example, assault a settlement from both east and west. Rarely attack the village via the gate. Not only is it stronger than a wall segment, your opponent is more likely to expect you there. Keep the element of surprise on your side by rarely "knocking on the front door."

These tips will have you well on your way to keeping the enemy at a distance or bringing down the house, depending on your objective. Good luck, fellow Empire builders.

Chapter Eleven

Multiplayer Empires

It's time to expand your empire. See if you can match wits with your friends. This chapter will help you get a handle on all the variables that must be considered when participating in multiplayer contests. Figure out which map and civilization are best for you, and then take your friends by storm.

Multiplayer Contest Preparations

After finishing the campaigns, you're probably ready for some multiplayer excitement. You can battle friends via direct connection, null modem, and the Internet. After hooking up, realize that several factors are important for success against flesh-and-blood opponents. Some of these are as follows:

- Latency, the time it takes information to travel from your computer to your opponents' computers, can adversely affect play with slide-show-quality movement. LAN (local area network) and serial connections offer the best latency. Internet-and-modem-connected contests have slower latency but are good for playing opponents who live several states away. The MSN Gaming Zone, by the way, is one of the best places to test your skills against the best.

- Understanding the advantages and disadvantages of each civilization is critical for winning. The "Civilizations at a Glance" section in this chapter is geared toward helping you understand each Empire's strengths and weaknesses, and it provides tips for choosing game types and determining player experience levels.

- Knowing the characteristics of each map and how they are conducive to your civilization's attributes is important. A brief summary of all 18 maps is featured in the "New Maps" section. The best types of maps for each civilization are listed in the "Civilizations at a Glance" section.

Note: *See Chapter 18 of* Microsoft Age of Empires II: The Age of Kings: Inside Moves *(Microsoft Press, 1999) for tips on decreasing latency as well as in-depth multiplayer tactics involving Random Map, Regicide, and Death Match contests.*

These three factors are important considerations for those seeking multiplayer bliss.

Civilizations at a Glance

Aztecs

- **Civilization Type:**   Infantry and Monk
- **Unique Unit:**   Jaguar Warrior (anti-infantry unit)
- **Unique Technology:**   Garland Wars (+4 infantry attacks and +6 attack bonus vs. Cavalry)

Strengths

- Infantry
- Monks
- Economy

Weaknesses

- Cavalry
- Navy
- Few gunpowder units

Tips

- **Recommended Player Experience Level:**   Expert
- **Recommended Game Types:**   Random Map (Relics victory) and Wonder Race
- **Recommended Map Types:**   Land-based

Note: The Aztecs have serious drawbacks on both land and sea. First of all, they have no Cavalry units. Furthermore, the Mesoamerican empire sports the game's worst navy. The key to winning thus lies with early attacks involving your Archers, Skirmishers, and Infantry. (See Figure 11-1.) Aztec Monks, the most powerful monks in the game, are especially important for grabbing Relics and healing the wounded. Try to win early. Generally, the longer a match lasts, the worse your chances are.

Figure 11-1 *Players commanding the Aztecs need to be aggressive with a capital "A."*

Britons

- **Civilization Type:** Foot Archer
- **Unique Unit:** Longbowman (Archer). See Figure 11-2 for an example of the Longbowman in action.
- **Unique Technology:** Yeoman (+1 Archer range and +2 tower attack)

Strengths

- Infantry
- Archers

Weaknesses

- Cavalry
- Siege
- Few gunpowder units

Figure 11-2   *With their long range, Longbowmen are one of the most effective units in the Britons' military arsenal.*

Tips

- **Recommended Player Experience Level:**   Mid-Level
- **Recommended Game Types:**   Random Map (Relics or Wonder victory), Wonder Race, and Defend the Wonder (defending)
- **Recommended Map Types:**   Land-based or water-based

Note: Are you ready for the good news and bad news? The bad news, which isn't all that bad, is that British Town Centers now cost 50 percent less Wood *only* during the Castle Age. On the bright side, though, Yeoman technology improves Archer range and Tower attacks. Now with all available technologies researched, a British Arbalest, for example, has a firing distance of 9—a range greater than that of an ordinary Siege Onager and Bombard Tower.

Byzantines

- **Civilization Type:** Defensive
- **Unique Unit:** Cataphract (anti-infantry Cavalry unit)
- **Unique Technology:** Logistica (Cataphracts inflict trample damage)

Strengths

- Infantry
- Archers
- Cavalry
- Navy
- Gunpowder units

Weaknesses

- Siege weapons

Tips

- **Recommended Player Experience Level:** Novice
- **Recommended Game Types:** Random Map (Relics, Wonder, Time Limit, or Score victory), Regicide, King of the Hill, and Defend the Wonder (defending)
- **Recommended Map Types:** Land-based or water-based

Note: The Byzantines are one of only nine civilizations with the new Halberdier. Furthermore, the unit costs –25 percent of what is required of other cultures. The Halberdier is an infantry unit effective against Cavalry, especially War Elephants. (See Figure 11-3.) His presence here, along with the Byzantines' strong Cavalry, infantry, and Archers, creates one of the most potent armies in the game.

Celts

- **Civilization Type:** Infantry
- **Unique Unit:** Woad Raider (fast antibuilding infantry unit)
- **Unique Technology:** Furor Celtica (Siege Workshops produce units with 50 percent more Hit Points)

Figure 11-3   *Use Halberdiers to protect Archers from enemy Cavalry units.*

Strengths

- Infantry
- Cavalry
- Siege weapons

Weaknesses

- Archers
- Monks
- Few gunpowder units

Tips

- **Recommended Player Experience Level:** Mid-Level
- **Recommended Game Types:** Random Map (Conquest, Wonder, Time Limit, or Score victory), King of the Hill, Wonder Race, and Defend the Wonder (attacking)
- **Recommended Map Types:** Land-based or water-based

Note: The addition of the Hussar complements the Celts' strong Cavalry, while Furor Celtica technology makes the civilization's powerful siege weapons all the more durable. The Celts still have some major drawbacks in the Archery, Monk (as shown in Figure 11-4), and gunpowder departments, though. These can be overcome with strategies implementing numerous rushes and blitzes.

Figure 11-4   *Celtic Monks are some of the weakest in the game, with the ability to research and use only half of the Monastery technologies.*

Chinese

- **Civilization Type:**   Archer
- **Unique Unit:**   Chu Ko Nu (fast, multifiring crossbowman)
- **Unique Technology:**   Rocketry (+2 Chu Ko Nu pierce attack, +4 scorpions). See Figure 11-5.

Strengths

- Infantry
- Archers
- Cavalry

Weaknesses

- Siege weapons

Tips

- **Recommended Player Experience Level:** Novice
- **Recommended Game Types:** Random Map (all types), Regicide, King of the Hill, and Defend the Wonder (defending)
- **Recommended Map Types:** Land-based or water-based

Note: Although the Chinese now start with greater Wood and Food debts, the civilization's military strength is slightly improved with the Rocketry technology. This aids an ailing siege weapon department with +4 Scorpion attacks. The fast-flinging Chu Ko Nu's increase in pierce attacks is helpful against opponents' Blacksmith upgrades and a load of units now equipped with piercing armor (Swordsmen, Berserks, Huskarls, Samurai, and Woad Raiders).

Figure 11-5 *Rocketry technology offers much-needed support for the Chinese's poor siege arsenal.*

Franks

- **Civilization Type:** Cavalry
- **Unique Unit:** Axeman (ranged antibuilding infantry)
- **Unique Technology:** Bearded Axe (+1 Throwing Axeman range)

Strengths

- Infantry
- Cavalry
- Navy

Weaknesses

- Archers
- No high-tier towers
- Economy

Tips

- **Recommended Player Experience Level:**   Mid-Level
- **Recommended Game Types:**   Random Map (all types), King of the Hill, and Defend the Wonder (defending)
- **Recommended Map Types:**   Land-based or water-based with high amounts of resources

Note: The Franks have improved unique unit abilities. Bearded Axe technology improves the Throwing Axeman's range +1. (See Figure 11-6.) This equals the firing distance of Skirmishers, Archers, Heavy Cavalry Archers, Chu Ko Nu, and Manguoai, which is significant for a civilization with weak Archery Range units.

Figure 11-6   *Improved Throwing Axeman range makes the unique unit more effective against Archers and Skirmishers.*

Goths

- **Civilization Type:** Infantry
- **Unique Unit:** Huskarl (anti-Archer infantry)
- **Unique Technologies:** Anarchy (Barracks can create Huskarls) and Perfusion (Barracks produce units 50 percent faster)

Strengths

- Infantry
- Archers
- Navy
- Economy

Weaknesses

- Defenses
- Cavalry
- Siege weapons
- Monks

Tips

- **Recommended Player Experience Level:** Expert
- **Recommended Game Types:** Random Map (Conquest or Time Limit victory), King of the Hill, and Defend the Wonder (attacking)
- **Recommended Map Types:** Land-based or water-based, especially one with lots of forests that can be used as defensive barriers

Note: The Goths are a much-improved lot. Besides having a +5 attack against Wild Boar, Hunters now carry +15 meat. Goths also are the only civilization with two unique technologies. Both Perfusion and Anarchy enable Goth lovers to get the most out of their Huskarls. (See Figure 11-7.) Huskarls are multitalented demolition machines, great against other infantry as well as Cavalry and Archers. Other than Skirmishers, they are, of course, the only unit with attack bonuses against Archers. Huskarls also have attack bonuses against buildings.

Figure 11-7   *The Huskarl is one of the strongest melee units in the game. Only two Castle Age infantry units, the Woad Raider and Teutonic Knight, have more attack points.*

Huns

- **Civilization Type:**   Cavalry
- **Unique Unit:**   Tarkan (antibuilding Cavalry)
- **Unique Technology:**   Atheism (+100 years Wonder/Relic victory time and 50 percent Spies/Treason cost)

Strengths

- Cavalry
- Navy
- Economy

Weaknesses

- Defenses
- Monks
- Few gunpowder units

Tips

- **Recommended Player Experience Level:** Novice
- **Recommended Game Types:** Random Map (all types), Regicide, King of the Hill, Wonder Race, and Defend the Wonder (attacking)
- **Recommended Map Types:** Land-based or water-based

Note: The Huns are a powerful war machine. Although referred to as a Cavalry civilization, they have strong infantry and archery attributes. Cavalry Archers benefit from cost reductions in the Castle and Imperial Age. Huns have access to all Barracks' technologies and units, except for the Champion, Eagle Warrior, and Elite Eagle Warrior. Besides the Tarkan, the Huns have three other new expansion pack units (the Halberdier, Hussar, and Petard), and they don't have to build Houses for their Villagers. (See Figure 11-8.) Moreover, Atheism is extremely useful in Regicide, Wonder, and Relic contests.

Figure 11-8   *The Huns have access to most economic technologies. Perhaps, though, their greatest economic strength lies in not having to build Houses.*

Japanese

- **Civilization Type:** Infantry
- **Unique Unit:** Samurai (antiunique unit infantry). See Figure 11-9.
- **Unique Technology:** Kataparuto (Trebuchets fire and unpack or pack faster)

Strengths

- Infantry
- Archers
- Navy
- Monks

Weaknesses

- Cavalry
- Siege weapons
- Economy
- Building technologies

Tips

- **Recommended Player Experience Level:** Mid-Level
- **Recommended Game Types:** Random Map (Conquest, Relic, Time Limit, or Score victory), and Death Match
- **Recommended Map Types:** Water-based or land-based maps with lots of resources

Note: The Japanese have a number of strengths; however, they are most adept on water-based maps due to their poor combination of weaknesses. Improvements in Samurai speed and attack bonuses against unique units, however, benefit the Japanese more in land battles, as does Kataparuto technology. The Fishing Ships' work rate and cost reductions for Mills, Lumber Camps, and Mining Camps aid the Japanese's fledgling economy somewhat. The civilization's Monks are extremely strong, with only one unavailable Monastery technology, making Relic victories an especially nice option on land-based maps.

Figure 11-9   *Samurai not only have more speed, but the Uji warriors have increased attack bonuses vs. unique units.*

Koreans

- **Civilization Type:**   Tower and Naval
- **Unique Units:**   War Wagon (Cavalry Archer) and Turtle Ship (heavily armored war vessel). See Figure 11-10.
- **Unique Technology:**   Shinkichon (+2 Mangonel range)

Strengths

- Defenses
- Infantry
- Archers
- Navy
- Economy

Weaknesses

- Cavalry
- Monks

Tips

- **Recommended Player Experience Level:** Novice
- **Recommended Game Types:** Random Map (all types), Regicide, King of the Hill, Wonder Race, and Defend the Wonder (defending)
- **Recommended Map Types:** Land-based and water-based

Note: The Koreans are one of the best all-around civilizations in *The Conquerors Expansion*. They have two powerful unique units, with economic, offensive, and defensive strongpoints. In particular, the Korean civilization's unique technology aids it in the siege weapons department. Korean Monks are not stellar, but they are quite capable with six of the ten Monastery technologies available. Korean Cavalry are not a liability, but they are hampered by mediocrity. Although most Stable units are available, the inability to research Bloodlines can be problematic at times. Overall, though, the Koreans are good at all game types and all maps—the optimum choice for beginners.

Figure 11-10 *Elite War Wagons are fast and highly durable Archers. As far as mobile land units go, only the Elite War Elephant and War Elephant have more Hit Points.*

AGE
of
EMPIRES II

Mayans

- **Civilization Type:** Archer
- **Unique Unit:** Plumed Archer (powerful foot Archer)
- **Unique Technology:** El Dorado (Eagle Warriors have +40 Hit Points)

Strengths

- Infantry
- Archers
- Monks
- Navy

Weaknesses

- Cavalry
- Few gunpowder units

Tips

- **Recommended Player Experience Level:** Expert
- **Recommended Game Types:** Random Map (Relics or Time Limit victory), Wonder Race, and Defend the Wonder (defending)
- **Recommended Map Types:** Land-based or water-based

Note: Along with the Aztecs, the Mayans are one of the most difficult civilizations for novices to command in Random Map contests. No Stable units and few gunpowder-related units make winning difficult in the latter Ages. The Mayans, however, have a strong arsenal of Archers and infantry. (See Figure 11-11.) You must—to win—use aggressive tactics, taking advantage of the civilization's superiority in the early stages of a game. Badgering your opponent with constant attacks as well as destroying enemy economic structures are necessary when playing as the Mayans.

Figure 11-11   *The Mayans are one of only two civilizations that begin contests with an Eagle Warrior. This infantry unit is faster and more durable, and delivers stronger attacks than the Scout Cavalry.*

Mongols

- **Civilization Type:** Cavalry Archer
- **Unique Unit:** Mangudai (anti-siege weapon Cavalry Archer)
- **Unique Technology:** Drill (Siege weapons move 50 percent faster)

Strengths

- Infantry
- Archers
- Cavalry
- Siege weapons
- Navy

Weaknesses

- Monks
- Defenses
- No high-tier towers
- Economy
- Few gunpowder units

Tips

- **Recommended Player Experience Level:** Mid-Level
- **Recommended Game Types:** Random Map (Conquest, Time Limit, or Score victory), Death Match, King of the Hill, and Defend the Wonder (attacking)
- **Recommended Map Types:** Land-based or water-based with high resources

Note: The Mongols are one of the most aggressive civilizations in *Microsoft Age of Empires II*. They are strong in all military departments: infantry, Cavalry, Archers, siege weaponry, and navy. Coupled with the new Hussar, Mongolian Mangudai are especially powerful units, great for taking out infantry units, siege weapons, Monks, and Persian War Elephants. (See Figure 11-12.) Overall, the Mongols are for people who attack their opponent just minutes after the bell rings. A weak Farming economy and poor building defenses, however, make falling behind

Figure 11-12 *The Mongol Mangudai are now even more potent with Hussars in the front line.*

easy in long-term battles. New Monk technologies and the Castle's Drill, though, are a big help. All in all, Mongols are an excellent answer against civilizations that rely heavily on Monks or siege weapons or both, such as the Celts, Saracens, and Teutons.

Persians

- **Civilization Type:**   Cavalry
- **Unique Unit:**   War Elephant (powerful but slow antibuilding Cavalry unit)
- **Unique Technology:**   Mahouts (War Elephants move 30 percent faster)

Strengths

- Cavalry
- Navy
- Economy

Weaknesses

- Infantry
- Monks
- Defenses

Tips

- **Recommended Player Experience Level:**   Novice
- **Recommended Game Types:**   Random Map (Conquest), King of the Hill, Wonder Race, and Defend the Wonder (attacking)
- **Recommended Map Types:**   Land-based or water-based

Note: The Persians are, in essence, a civilization of brute power. They have a Cavalry juggernaut, complete with all Stable units and technologies. Moreover, they have the most durable *Age of Empires II* mobile unit, the War Elephant—which has just gotten faster (when Mahouts is researched; see Figure 11-13). Ensemble Studios has made a number of other enhancements to the Persians. The civilization now has Petards, Halberdiers, and Hussars in its arsenal. Archers are strengthened with the new Thumb Ring and Parthian Tactics technologies. The Persians are an ideal civilization that can hold its own against any opponent, even the Mongols and Saracens.

Figure 11-13 *Mahouts increases the pace of the staggeringly slow Persian War Elephant.*

Saracens

- **Civilization Type:** Camel and Naval
- **Unique Unit:** Mameluke (ranged anti-Cavalry Camel unit)
- **Unique Technology:** Zealotry (Camels and Mamelukes have +30 Hit Points)

Strengths

- Infantry
- Archers
- Cavalry
- Monks
- Navy

Weaknesses

- Economy
- Building technologies

Tips

- **Recommended Player Experience Level:**   Novice
- **Recommended Game Types:**   Random Map (all types), King of the Hill, and Defend the Wonder (attacking)
- **Recommended Map Types:**   Land-based or water-based with high amounts of resources

Note: Launching your jihad has become even easier with stronger Saracen Camels, Mamelukes, and Monks. Not only do Camels and Heavy Camels move quicker (as shown in Figure 11-14), Zealotry increases their Hit Points. Overall, Mamelukes and Camels are formidable opposition for other Cavalry-based civilizations. The Saracens also have access to all new non-civilization-specific technologies. The civilization, however, is still plagued by its lackluster economy and poor supply of building technologies at the Castle and University. Trading is a good idea, especially since Market Trade is cheaper. Teaming up with civilizations such as the Mayans, Aztecs, and Goths (cultures with strong economies) is also something to consider.

Figure 11-14   *Saracen Camels become stronger than those in other civilizations when you research Zealotry.*

Spanish

- **Civilization Type:**   Gunpowder and Monk
- **Unique Units:**   Conquistador (mounted Hand Cannoneer) and Missionary (mounted Monk)
- **Unique Technology:**   Supremacy (Villagers more effective in combat)

Strengths

- Infantry
- Cavalry
- Navy
- Monks (See Figure 11-15.)
- Defenses
- Gunpowder units

Weaknesses

- Archers
- Siege weapons

Tips

- **Recommended Player Experience Level:**   Novice
- **Recommended Game Types:**   Random Map (all types), Death Match, Regicide, King of the Hill, Wonder Race, and Defend the Wonder (attacking)
- **Recommended Map Types:**   Land-based or water-based

Note: The Spanish are one of the strongest civilizations in *Age of Empires II*. They have access to all Monk, Cavalry, infantry, and naval technologies. Moreover, they have every gunpowder-related unit in the game as well as two powerful unique units. The Spanish's only weakness is a poor selection of Archers. The civilization's siege arsenal is just mediocre, due primarily to the absence of the Siege Onager and lack of Siege Engineers technology.

Figure 11-15 *Missionaries do not have as high a range as Monks do, but their speed is greater.*

Teutons

- **Civilization Type:** Infantry
- **Unique Unit:** Teutonic Knight (slow but powerful antibuilding infantry unit). See Figure 11-16.
- **Unique Technology:** Crenellations (+3 Castle range and garrisoned infantry fire arrows)

Strengths

- Infantry
- Gunpowder units
- Siege weapons
- Monks
- Defenses

Weaknesses

- Archers
- Cavalry

Tips

- **Recommended Player Experience Level:**   Mid-Level
- **Recommended Game Types:**   Random Map (Relic victory), Regicide, King of the Hill, Defend the Wonder (defending)
- **Recommended Map Types:**   Land-based

Note: If you're looking for a strong land-based civilization consistent throughout the Ages, the Teutons are for you. They have a strong economy and powerful defenses, and are capable of mounting impressive offensive fronts. Bloodlines strengthen the culture's Cavalry units, making Stable units less of a weakness than before. Archery Range units are still a major liability.

The Hand Cannoneer is a nice consolation, though, especially since the Teutons have the economic strength to advance quickly to the Imperial Age. A more problematic area for this Germanic tribe, though, lies in the naval department. The lack of Dry Dock and Shipwright technologies, along with the lack of Elite Cannon Galleons, are tough to overcome in long battles on water-based maps.

Figure 11-16   *Teutonic Knights and Crenallations often put the Teutons over the top during the Castle Age.*

Turks

- **Civilization Type:** Gunpowder
- **Unique Unit:** Janissary (powerful Hand Cannoneer). See Figure 11-17.
- **Unique Technology:** Artillery (Bombard Towers, Bombard Cannons, and Cannon Galleons have +2 range)

Strengths

- Cavalry
- Navy
- Gunpowder units
- Defenses

Weaknesses

- Archers
- Monks
- Siege weapons

Tips

- **Recommended Player Experience Level:** Novice
- **Recommended Game Types:** Random Map (Conquest, Wonder, Time Limit, or Score victory), Regicide, King of the Hill, and Defend the Wonder (defending)
- **Recommended Map Types:** Land-based or water-based

Note: A horde of new features strengthen this *Age of Empires II* power-house. Besides a 25 percent increase in Hit Points, all major gunpowder units see either an increase in attack points or firing range. The free Hussar upgrade is an additional advantage. Since Turkish Barracks and Archery Range units are lackluster, use the available technologies at the Blacksmith to upgrade these units. Furthermore, use the Towers to defend your resources, especially Gold mines.

Figure 11-17   *The Janissary's attack points have increased +2, while the Elite Janissary's attack points have been raised +4.*

Vikings

- **Civilization Type:**   Infantry and Naval
- **Unique Units:**   Berserk (self-healing antibuilding infantry unit) and Longboat (powerful war ship)
- **Unique Technology:**   Berserkergang (Beserks heal quicker)

Strengths

- Infantry
- Navy (See Figure 11-18.)
- Building technologies

Weaknesses

- Cavalry
- Monks
- No high-tier towers
- Few gunpowder units

Tips

- **Recommended Player Experience Level:** Expert
- **Recommended Game Types:** Random Map (Conquest or Time Limit victory), Wonder Race, and Defend the Wonder (attacking)
- **Recommended Map Types:** Water-based

Note: The Vikings are one of the most difficult civilizations to command due to a significant deficiency of Castle and Imperial Age technology and units—unless you're on a water-based map, where this civilization really shines. Mighty Odin's troops unfortunately are still burdened with one of the weakest Cavalry and Monks in the game. However, increases in infantry Hit Points and faster-healing Berserkers (a definite plus considering the weak clerics) add to their strength in land battles. The Vikings also have plentiful building technologies like Masonry and Murder Holes, useful in defending villages. Overall, though, the strong infantry is best used in water-based battles, in which it can be dispatched in Transport Ships for surprise attacks.

Figure 11-18   *Viking Longboats, due to their range, speed, and Hit Points, are excellent for battling Fire Ships and Galleys.*

New Maps

A total of 18 new maps are available. New Standard Maps and Real World Maps cater to a variety of tactics and civilizations. Along with your experience level and civilization, the type of map you choose is critical to your success in multiplayer battles. Here's a brief rundown of the new maps.

New Standard Map Styles

Eight new standard maps are included in *The Conquerors Expansion* pack. These include terrain featuring snow and frozen lakes as well as new indigenous life forms such as Wild Turkeys and Jaguars. Most of these maps cater to civilizations with strong armies. With the exception of Salt Marsh, extensive naval capabilities are not stressed.

> **Note:** *Selecting Random Land Map results in a random selection of one of the following maps: Arabia, Ghost Lake, Highland, Mongolia, Oasis, or Yucatan.*

Arena

You can't run—or hide. Arena is strictly a land map with lush forests surrounding the civilizations. Only the ready-built Walls protect each player from immediate attack. Although there's quite a bit of room for building structures inside your fortress, you'll need to advance outside the Walls to obtain Gold, Food, Stone, and Relics. Establishing a smaller fortress in the center of the map is important for mounting serious attacks on your opponents, as it cuts down the distance your siege units must travel. Strong hard-hitting civilizations, such as the Persians, Spanish, Teutons, and Turks, are ideal for Arena battles.

Ghost Lake

Ghost Lake contains a frozen lake in the center of the map, full of small scattered forests and cliffs. Although you can't build structures on the icy lake, troops can traverse the arctic terrain, allowing you to attack from all fronts. Use the snow to track your enemies. Attack early and consistently to be successful. Moreover, construct Walls to seal your village from numerous assaults.

Mongolia

Mongolia is a barren landscape of sand, cliffs, and scattered forests. This map requires a lot of exploration due to the terrain type. Quickly navigate toward the center of the map and establish forces there. An extensive maze of cliffs make chokepoint defenses highly effective. They also provide additional protection for your Archers and ranged siege weapons. The Britons, Chinese, Mongols, and Saracens fare well on Mongolia.

Nomad

Nomad consists of a huge peninsula (sometimes tropical and sometimes arctic), full of small patches of forest. Invest in a navy because you'll need the fish to

support your Food count. Don't go overboard with the war ships, though. A strong army will be absolutely necessary for victory. The Byzantines, Japanese, Koreans, Persians, Spanish, and Turks are some of the best-equipped civilizations for handling this map.

Oasis

The oasis rests in center of this map; it's a small pond surrounded by a thick forest of Palm trees. Erect your village in one of the corners. Place Lumber Camps near the map's center to obtain a rich and steady source of Wood. Protect your Camps with plenty of Towers. Attack your opponent's resource sites, concentrating on less plentiful resources such as Gold and Stone. Implement "squeeze" assaults—attacking from around both sides of the Oasis. Since your opponent knows not to expect attacks coming through the map's center, don't add to the predictability factor by attacking a base from just one side.

Salt Marsh

The Salt Marsh is primarily swampy terrain, consisting of numerous river inlets and marshes. Amphibious combat and strategies are a must here. You'll need a capable army and navy to take control of the map. Build Docks early, focusing on catching fish and transporting Villagers. Remember that marshes are important chokepoints, so be ready with Walls, Towers, and siege equipment. Explore the entirety of this map because you want to know where opponents are and what possibilities they have for invading your territory—which are usually many.

Scandinavia

Scandinavia is not the familiar shape of Norway, Sweden, and Finland, but it features the terrain of those areas. Cliffs, forests, and small frozen ponds are scattered on snow-clad terrain, while fjords run parallel on two edges of the map. The thin strips of water are best for obtaining fish. Don't invest heavily in an armed navy, unless you feel you must repel numerous opponents from the Food source. Large Walled structures are difficult to erect due to the frozen lakes and cliffs; thus, use the cliffs for stationing Archers, siege equipment, and Towers. But don't sit back; consistently hammering opponents is necessary on this map.

Yucatan

The Yucatan was the home of the Mayans. Like Scandinavia, this map is not shaped into a peninsula but features the terrain characteristics of that area. Small strewn lakes and thick forests fill the landscape—along with man-hungry Jaguars. Use the lakes and forest chokepoints for defensive maneuvers. Moreover, station Trebuchets and siege equipment behind thin stretches of forest and pummel enemies as they navigate through the region. Guerilla warfare of all sorts works well in this setting.

Real World Map Styles

Real World Maps apply the shapes and terrain of real-world locations. For example, Britain contains the British Isle along with Ireland, the northern edge of France (Normandy), and part of Norway. The rocky cliffs of Dover and lush countryside of France are depicted in a simplistic yet semirealistic manner. A variety of Real World Maps are at your disposal, including Byzantium, Central America, and the Sea of Japan.

Britain

The Britain map contains the British Isle, Ireland, Normandy, and the western tip of Norway. If on Britain, form some Walls with the cliffs along the southeastern and northeastern coasts of the Isle. This will prevent attacks from Norman and Norwegian invaders, allowing you to focus your attention on civilizations stationed in Ireland. If starting on another area of the map, quickly land on Britain, build up forces, and gather resources. Controlling this island and spanning outward is the best course for victory. A strong navy, of course, is vital to doing this.

Byzantium

After Rome fell, the eastern part of the Empire continued on for several hundred years. Byzantium spanned from the Greek peninsula to the peninsula of Anatolia. A strong navy and defense are important due to the various water systems running through this region. Begin your conquest by first taking one of the two peninsulas, eventually invading the other by at least the early Castle Age. Also, take control of the sea early with lots of Docks. Demolition Ships, Cannon Galleons, and Turtle Ships are effective on the seas. Demolition Ships are good for battling hordes of attacking Galleons, which often bunch up in the bays and inlets.

Central America

This map consists of Central America as well as the southeastern stretch of North America. Establishing a navy is essential for catching fish and defending or

attacking the coastal areas, which are where most trees and resources are located. Use Galleons and their upgraded versions, with their long range, to control the Central American region. Dominate North America with your land units. The Japanese, Koreans, Mayans, Mongols, Saracens, Spanish, and Vikings perform well on this map.

France

France consists of not only France but also the northeastern part of Spain and the southern tip of Britain. Watch out for invaders from Spain since the Pyrenees are absent in this representation. Civilizations with weak navies can win on this map by taking out any enemy villages on Britain early, and then concentrating forces on the mainland. Don't hide behind Walls; be aggressive. Resources are fairly plentiful, but use Towers to defend your Camps from enemy assaults.

Iberia

Iberia contains the Iberian peninsula (Spain and Portugal) as well as a narrow stretch of North Africa. Iberia is vulnerable to naval invasions from all areas, except the northeast. Two large river inlets into Spain make things even worse for Iberian defenders. A strong, dominant navy is a major key here. Squashing the opposition early, or at least lording over the map's resources, is an important tactic for victory. Civilizations with potent Dock units and technologies, such as the Japanese, Koreans, Saracens, Spanish, and Vikings, are geared best for this.

Italy

Italy is another map that caters heavily to naval powers. Cliffs, representing the Alps, prevent land forces from sweeping into Italy from the north. This enables civilizations on the boot-shaped peninsula to concentrate defenses and attacks on the Baltic and North African coasts. If starting on Italy, taking out surrounding forces early is critical; otherwise, you'll be sandwiched with constant assaults.

Mideast

The Mideast comprises Middle East territory. Dominating the Arabian peninsula is essential due to the abundance of resources there. However, defending this region can be difficult without both naval and land-based units. Watch out for invaders from the west (ancient Egypt) and the east (ancient Persia). As with most Real World Maps, whoever controls the sea wins. Overall, the Byzantines, Huns, Persians, Saracens, Spanish, and Turks perform particularly well on this map.

Norse Lands

The Norse Lands consists of snow-clad representations of Norway, Sweden, Finland, Denmark, and Holland. Controlling Norway enables you to attack and exploit other regions of the map. Narrow and quick Viking Longboats and Fire Ships are particularly agile in the sea, where sheets of ice make navigation difficult.

Sea of Japan (East Sea)

The Japanese and Koreans can re-create their famous naval battles on this map. Dominating the East Sea is important for developing a strong fishing trade, which is a necessary Food source for staying competitive. Establishing beachheads near your enemies is also a key to victory. If stationed on the Korean peninsula, surprise the civilization on Japan by attacking the eastern side of the island. As always, multifront assaults make taking down opponents much easier.

Texas

Although Texas is represented as a large island-continent surrounded by water, land battles are usually the decisive factor in winning the Lone Star. The lack of river inlets reduces the role of navies to basically just fishing for Food. Attack opponents nearest your settlement first, concentrating on their economic structures. Meanwhile, keep a close eye on other civilizations via your Eagle Warrior or Scout Cavalry. Civilizations ideal for this map include the Celts, Goths, Huns, Mongols, Persians, and Teutons.

PART III

Inside Moves: Information You Won't Find Anywhere Else

Chapter Twelve

The BattleBits

The BattleBits are unique to this strategy guide. Think of them as small missions. But they are missions with a point—to teach some of the battle concepts of *Microsoft Age of Empires II*. Don't confuse these missions with the game's tutorials. While the tutorials do an excellent job of teaching you how to play the game, BattleBits will teach you how to fight—and win.

The following are descriptions of the ten BattleBits. The BattleBits themselves can be easily downloaded from the Microsoft Press Web site at *http:// mspress.microsoft.com/mspress/products/4782/*. You can download all ten (less than 10 megabytes), or you can download them individually.

Each BattleBit on the Web site expands on one of the following descriptions and includes a printable document that explains how to beat the 'Bit if it gives you trouble. So without out further ado, read on to see what the 'Bits are all about.

Nowhere to Go

As is often the case in *Age of Empires II,* this BattleBit asks you to defeat—by elimination—a superior force. There are no resources to be mined or reinforcements to be gained. It's just you against them, and there's no outside assistance. Or is there? Help can come from the least expected quarters, even those who know not whom they help.

> **Tip:** *Look to the terrain for the answer. Your Archers need to be kept out of harm's way to work their magic. What might help you accomplish this?*

One Thing at a Time

Ahead lies a massive Teuton army, and beyond them the Castle that you must raze. The Teutons easily outnumber your Franks, and you have no long-range

> **Tip:** *Going head to head with the Teutons can be suicide, but only if you put all of your heads against all of their heads at the same time. Perhaps there is a way to isolate a portion of their army....*

weapons with which to bombard them from afar. How can you defeat the Teuton army and destroy their Castle?

Read My Lips. It's the...

Age of Empires II—like other real-time strategy titles—is primarily a game of economics. More often than not the civilization with the most powerful economy will win any given mission. The goal here is simple: be the first civilization to reach the economic status dictated in the BattleBit. To do so, you must not only use the Hun civilization's strengths effectively, but....

> **Tip:** *Remember, each race must have at least two contestants. It's not necessary to move quickly to win a race, just less slowly than your competition.*

To Catch an Arrow

> **Tip:** *The trouble with Archers is arrows, or at least how long they have to pump your soldiers' bodies full of quilled shafts. Is there perhaps a way to limit the time spent receiving shafts?*

The Christian Archers have the high ground. For days they have rained their deadly shafts on you. Your swordsmen have repeatedly assailed the line of Knights that covers their front, but to no avail. You must get through; it's your duty to break the siege of Ranuman. But how?

Everywhere at Once

> **Tip:** *Unlike the '80s pop-rock band the Plimsouls, you can't be everywhere at once. But is that really necessary?*

Your Koreans are magnificent builders of Towers and Keeps, but their ring of static defenses may not be enough against the foes they now face. Surrounded by Japanese on all sides, the Koreans must protect their Wonder or die trying.

Retrieval of Honor

Deep in the barbarians' camp lies the armor of your slain leader, Beadorn. For generations the clan leader's armor has been passed down to the next birthright. Now, the clawed ones, those of the FireSnake, have killed Beadorn and stolen his armor. It's up to your band of Vikings to retrieve the armor.

Tip: *A straight-up assault looks risky. Could there be another way?*

Trouble Ahead, Trouble Behind

Chased by Conquistadors, your Aztecs are on the run. Rumor has it that the Spanish have set an ambush ahead. Somehow, your men must fight their way through the Spanish armies and reach the reinforcements that wait to the south.

Tip: *There are three ways to attack a problem: you can go over it, around it, or through it. Which works best here?*

Bringing Down the House

Besieged on all sides, your Saracens wait behind their fortified walls. Outside, the Crusaders inexorably advance their siege weapons. The Saracens have no answers to the Christians' Trebuchets. It seems impossible to hold out until reinforcements arrive. Do you have any ideas?

Tip: *The lines between offense and defense can often become blurred. What might stop the Christians' Trebuchets and Rams?*

The Choices We Make

The runner says that hordes of Aztec warriors are marching on your village. You have little time and few resources to prepare for the upcoming battle. The decisions you make before the battle is joined will decide the outcome of the upcoming struggle. Where do you place your precious time and money?

Tip: *To win this BattleBit, you must apply several diverse pieces of knowledge. What are your strengths? What are your opponent's strengths? Where is the terrain most favorable to you?*

Final Exam

The armies are drawn up. The time for production is over. The general who conquers will be the one who best employs his troops. This is a no-holds-barred, large battle. You'll need to understand the opponent's warriors and the best use of terrain and formations to win. Good luck.

Tip: *Look for help in unexpected places. Once again, you must use terrain wisely in order to win.*

These BattleBits don't cover every tactical situation. A game as rich as *Age of Empires II: The Conquerors Expansion* has far too many possibilities to cover in ten BattleBits. The good news is that if you like these, there's no reason we can't do more later.

Chapter Thirteen

INSIDE TIPS

A strategy guide author has only limited time with any game. Accordingly, any help that he or she can garner is greatly appreciated. In this case, the help came from a most welcome source: a couple of the Microsoft Age II testers. These folks have lived, eaten, and breathed the game for the past several months. Take their answers to the questions below to heart.

Michael "Staffa" Christensen

Q. What is the strongest new civilization. Why?

A. Definitely the Mayans. They have a very powerful economy and a cheap, effective army, with a strong late-Imperial superunit.

Q. How do you suggest the Mayans and Aztecs compensate for their horseless civilization?

A. The Eagle Warrior takes the place of the mounted unit when it comes to taking out siege/ranged units. When it comes to something with a large number of hit points to take the hits, they don't have a replacement—they just have to make do with numbers instead of brawn.

Q. What is your favorite non-obvious tactic?

A. Large quantities of Skirmishers with Rams in the Castle Age. They are a very cheap army that can catch the opponent off guard. Thirty Elite Skimishers, a few Pikemen, and three Rams can wipe out an unprepared opponent very quickly.

Q. What—in one sentence—is the key to winning *Age of Empires II?*

A. Balance and adaptability.

Q. What is more important, quantity or quality?

A. Quantity, but quality should never be discounted.

Q. What is the most dangerous unit?

A. Mayan fully upgraded Elite Eagle Warrior.

Q. What does your favorite unit combination consist of?

A. Mayan Plumed Archers with Elite Eagle Warriors.

Q. What is the most important technology to research?

A. The Hand Cart.

Dennis Stone

Q. What is the strongest new civilization. Why?

A. For the expert player, Mayans are the strongest new civilization, the reason being they get the best economy bonus out of the new civilizations (and one of the best in the game). They also have a solid military in all ages and fully upgradeable cheap Archers, and the Mayan Eagle Warrior is deadly. The newer players will really like the Huns because they don't need houses, which makes micromanagement a bit easier throughout the game.

Q. How do you suggest the Mayans and Aztecs compensate for their horseless civilization?

A. When you aren't using stable units as a main part of your force, you usually just use stable units to take out siege weapons and Monks, and sometimes to raid your opponent's economy. The Mayans and Aztecs can do all of these things with their Eagle Warriors. They are quick, and they have high pierce armor and resistance to Monks.

Q. What is your favorite non-obvious attack?

A. An all-out Feudal attack involving Towers and Spearmen, with almost any civilization.

Q. What is the key to winning?

A. Hit first, hit hard, and don't let your economy go unattended while doing it.

Q. Which is more important, quantity or quality?

A. Neither one is more important than the other; what's really important is that you have the right mix. Having a ton of basic units might end up with you watching all your units die before you get your money's worth, but having all the upgrades might leave you with too small an army. In most situations, I'd go for quality first and then try to keep my units alive until I have quantity as well.

Q. What is the most dangerous unit?

A. The game is too well balanced in my opinion to pick a most dangerous unit overall. It really varies from situation to situation.

Q. What is your favorite unit combination?

A. Elite Longbowmen, Halberdiers, and Trebuchets. In more general situations, I like the ranged unit/Halberdiers/Trebuchets combination.

Q. What do you think is the most important technology?

A. That varies from civilization to civilization and from game to game. In every game, it's important to get all the economy upgrades—the earlier the better.

Matthew Scadding

Q. What is the strongest new civilization. Why?

A. This is one of those questions asked in many an interview I've done, and the answer really comes down to personal preference. "Strongest" can apply to so many maps. Each requires a different strategy to overcome the enemy and hence requires a different civilization. I would have to say the Huns are the strongest new land civilization. Their lack of need for houses gives them an edge right from the start. Their biggest asset is their Cavalry units; however, this is also their biggest downfall. As a Hun, you can raid an enemy town with Elite Tarkans and kill a castle before the enemy can even respond.

A. On the water side of things, the Spanish can be a very powerful civilization if the game goes to the Imperial age. A Spanish Cannon Galleon with ballistics can pick off a Scout moving perpendicular to the galleon.

Q. How do you suggest the Mayans and Aztecs compensate for their horseless civilization?

A. These civilizations are both heavily dependent upon the Eagle Warrior as their fast-moving unit. Because of this, they need to mine a lot of Gold. People should keep in mind that Eagle Warriors are fairly fragile until they are fully upgraded.

Q. What—in one sentence—is the key to winning *Age of Empires II*?

A. Never give up; never surrender!

Q. What is more important, quantity or quality?

A. Your best bet is to have both quantity and quality.

Q. What does your favorite unit combination consist of?

A. Halberdiers and Japanese Trebuchets. There's something very satisfying about killing enemy Archers with giant siege weapons and having enemy Cavalry units drop like flies to the Japanese Halberds.

Q. What's the most important technology to research?

A. Any upgrade you are planning on using is important. If you're going to be creating a mostly infantry army, you have to get the attack, defense, and speed upgrades. But as many players know, I'm a firm believer in a strong economy, so if you're mining Gold, you should get the Gold upgrade as soon as possible. If you're chopping Wood, upgrade your choppers, and so on.

Appendix

Web Sites (and Newsgroups) of the Conquerors

Microsoft Age of Empires II (*Age II*) has generated a phenomenal level of interest. From Texas to Tiawan, gamers are playing, talking, and creating Web sites about *Age of Empires II*. This appendix takes a look at some of the better sites and tells you a bit of what they're about.

Web Sites

http://www.microsoft.com/games/age2/

This is the official Microsoft Web site for Microsoft games. The site includes complete information on the game, reviews, screen shots, *Age II* videos, links, patches, and downloads. Additionally, you'll find the AVI files that units in the game use when replying to your mouse click. You can also order the game from this site.

http://www.aoe2.com

Another great site. These folks cover not only *Age II* but also the original *Age of Empires* and its add-on packs. The site includes links, downloads, and a forum. Especially interesting are the strategies. Although formatted like an army field manual, they're nonetheless interesting if a bit generic.

AGE
of
EMPIRES II

http://age.gamestats.com/age/index.shtml

This is the *Age of Empires* heaven. No, really, that's the name of the site. This one has an extensive database of documents (many of which I used in designing the BattleBits) to help scenario designers, a nice strategies section, links, and downloads (which include scenarios and campaigns).

http://aoe2.playnow.com.au/aoe2/

Named "The Coliseum," this is a fantastic site. It has downloads and forums, and it even hosts tournaments. Better still, the site is frequently updated. I know that this site will be all over *The Conquerors Expansion* when it's released.

http://www.ensemblestudios.com/

The home site of the developers. A solid site, geared toward supplying the latest news to *Age II* fans. This is the place to go to find out what's happening. They even have a newsletter you can subscribe to.

Newsgroups

The *Age of Empires* community consists of more than just Web sites. There are also newsgroups full of dedicated gamers who love to share their insight into the game. You'll need a newsreader to access the groups. We recommend Microsoft Outlook (of course) or Microsoft Outlook Express.

- alt.games.microsoft.age-of-empires   This is where you post questions and comments for *Age of Empires*.
- alt.games.microsoft.rise-of-rome   This is where you post questions and comments for *Age of Empires: The Rise of Rome*.
- alt.games.microsoft.age-of-kings   This is where you post questions and comments for *Age of Empires II: The Age of Kings*.
- alt.games.microsoft.zone   This is where you post general questions and comments for the MSN Gaming Zone.
- microsoft.public.ageofempires   This is another place to post questions and comments for *Age of Empires*.
- microsoft.public.games.zone.strategy   This is where you post questions and comments about Microsoft strategy games.

Index

Mark H. Walker

Mark "just some dude" Walker is a veteran designer and journalist in the gaming industry. He has written seven strategy guides on real-time and turn-based strategy games, including *Microsoft Age of Empires II, Total Annihilation: Kingdoms, Warcraft II: Beyond the Dark Portal*, and *M.A.X. 2*. Additionally, he has designed and published scenarios for *Steel Panthers I & II, Tanks: Wargame Construction Set, Empire II: the Art of War*, and numerous board games such as *Advanced Squad Leader* and *Battlefield: Europe*. A former naval officer, Mark now lives in rural Virginia with his wife of 14 years and their three children, three dogs, two cats, a triumvirate of hamsters, and a goat named Duchess.

The manuscript for this book was prepared and submitted to Microsoft Press in electronic form. Text files were prepared using Microsoft Word 2000. Pages were composed by Microsoft Press using Adobe PageMaker 6.52 for Windows, with text in Garamond and display type in Ultra Condensed Sans One and Helvetica Condensed Black. Composed pages were delivered to the printer as electronic prepress files.

Cover Mechanical
Methodologie, Inc.

Interior Graphic Artist
Joel Panchot

Principal Compositor
Carl Diltz

Principal Proofreader/Copy Editor
Crystal Thomas

Indexer
Rebecca Plunkett

OWNER REGISTRATION CARD

Register Today!

0-7356-1177-7

Return the bottom portion of this card to register today.

Microsoft® Age of Empires® II: The Conquerors Expansion: Inside Moves

FIRST NAME | MIDDLE INITIAL | LAST NAME

INSTITUTION OR COMPANY NAME

ADDRESS

CITY | STATE | ZIP

(   )

E-MAIL ADDRESS | PHONE NUMBER

U.S. and Canada addresses only. Fill in information above and mail postage-free.
Please mail only the bottom half of this page.

For information about Microsoft Press®
products, visit our Web site at
mspress.microsoft.com

Microsoft